DID I MAKE YOU

PROUD

Darion Knight

S.H.E. PUBLISHING, LLC

DID I MAKE YOU PROUD

Copyright © 2024 by Darion Knight

For information contact:

www.shepublishingllc.com

www.info@shepublishingllc.com

Library of Congress Control Number: 2024935654

ISBN:

978-1-964061-00-9 (hardback)

978-1-953163-99-8 (paperback)

First Edition: April 2024

10 9 8 7 6 5 4 3 2 1

DEDICATION

To Jillian and Olivia Knight: May this book stand as a testament to the love and inspiration you've given me. Jillian, your support has fueled my journey, and Olivia, your smile and spirit lights my path. With gratitude and love, I dedicate "Did I Make You Proud" to you both.

--Darion

CONTENTS

THE MARCH-IN:

An Introduction to My Story

TODAY IS AN ESPECIALLY HARD DAY FOR ME. I'm sitting at a church on the Southside of Chicago, near the neighborhood where I grew up. A member of the Omega Psi Phi fraternity is reading the eulogy of a great friend of mine. I have never been an overly emotional guy, but today I can't hold back the tears. You see, I'm at my friend Kevin's funeral, and I'm remembering how much Kevin meant to me. He was one of my mentors, someone who I could go to when I needed business advice or advice on any other subject. Kevin was someone who would always tell me what I needed to hear, not what I wanted to hear.

Our friendship started in an unconventional way. He is the father of Chancellor, one of my former gymnasts. Kevin wanted Chancellor to play football, but Chancellor wanted to do gymnastics. Kevin just did not understand the sport at all, and I used to laugh at how uncomfortable he would look while sitting and waiting for practice to be over (well, when he wasn't knocked out sleeping). But after Chancellor made the decision to stick with gymnastics, Kevin just kind of went with the flow. Chancellor started gymnastics with me at Beverly Gymnastics Center, and the family followed me to whatever gym I went to from the time Chancellor was six years old until he graduated from high school and went on to Penn State University. Kevin and his family, who are now like family to me, have been around from the days when I was still trying to figure out who I was, when I found my future wife, and when I started my journey to become a gymnastics gym owner.

But today I'm at his funeral, and I'm listening to his eulogy. I hear a phrase that really hits home. The speaker says, "What did you do between your dash?" What he is really asking is, "What did you do between the day you were born and the day you were laid to rest?" (Like what is listed on your headstone.) What did you do between those two dates, and how did you affect the people in your life? This phrase made me think about my life and what I have done, if anything, to make an impact on someone's life like Kevin did for me. I'm writing this book to give people a little insight on my life to this point, and to reflect on what I have done with my dash.

So who is Darion Knight? Today I am a forty-six-year-old Black male who grew up on the Southside of Chicago. I had more money than some of my friends and less than others, but my family was definitely poor. Unlike a lot of the stories that came out of my community, I had both my parents present for the most part. My parents were friends, then a married couple, then a divorced couple, but are now friends again. My mom's side of the family was close-knit until my grandfather (Daddy Mo') died. My dad's side of the family was also close, but I didn't really know a lot about his immediate siblings and their kids until I began writing this book.

I was a good kid growing up, but it didn't always stay that way. I was a pretty smart kid, but at some point, people decided that being smart wasn't cool, so being the cool kid won out sometimes. I remember knowing that the second and fourth quarters in school mattered the most, and I would pull up any grades to where they needed to be during that time of year. The neighborhoods that I grew up in were terrible. The things that I saw and heard growing up are things that no child should have to experience. I remember being taught as a child that when the shooting starts, you need to get down on the floor quickly and stay there until the shooting stops (*and there were many nights when this would happen*). You had to know what gangs were in what neighborhood and which way they wore their hats. You had to know how to deal with death, because there was a chance that someone you knew would get killed. I have many really close friends who were victims of street violence. This, along with being a Black boy doing gymnastics, forced me to learn how to hide my feelings and become really good at defending myself.

I don't think I could be considered a religious person, but I am very spiritual. I believe that God puts people in your life who will help guide you to the path that He has chosen for you. It took me a long time to realize this, but since I have, the trajectory of my life has been going upward like a rocket. While I was trying to figure this out, I felt like I was constantly hitting a brick wall. Although I had some money and materialistic things, I was empty inside. I was trying to find happiness, but it was nowhere to be found. What I did find was stress, heartache, loneliness, and poor mental health.

The people who He put in my life all served a purpose. There were my parents, who taught me right from wrong and to treat people the way that I want to be treated. Though, judging by some of the decisions that I have made, you couldn't tell that I was listening to my parents at all. I had my family and childhood friends, who all were important components of my life. There were my coaches, who taught me the skills that I needed to be successful in gymnastics, and I had a few of them. I couldn't see these lessons or understand these teachings for my future life until now, but I'll go into that a little bit later. Then I had the people who I met after my competitive gymnastics career. These are friends and associates who also helped shape who I am today. This started as a pretty dark period for me. This was a time of rebellion and confusion, but was also a time when I tried to figure out my new purpose.

This period of me trying to "figure it out" lasted for a long time, probably over twenty years. It took me that long to realize how much of an effect that losing gymnastics had on me. How losing family and friends at an early age added to my fragile mental state. How my parents' divorce when I was a young child affected me. This was also a time when I questioned God and why He would take my loved ones away (like my grandfather Daddy Mo'). Life didn't mean as much to me. I struggled with depression, alcoholism, and a loss of faith. No one around me knew any of this. All they saw was the Darion who loved to have a good time and would party and dance all night. Others knew the Darion who would fight in a second to protect friends and loved ones. Little did they know that inside, I was a shell of a man. The guy who was the life of the party was hiding the fact that inside, he was broken. The person who would protect his friends at any cost didn't really care about life that much.

The reason that I always had to have people around me was because when I was alone, I would think about all that I had lost. This masquerade that I was putting on was mostly because I am a people pleaser. I wanted to make everyone who was in my life proud. I wanted to make my parents proud by graduating from school and getting a good job. I also wanted to be able to live up to this image that my parents had of me. I wanted to make my gymnastics coaches proud by winning gymnastics competitions and trying to make the Olympics. Unfortunately, I didn't accomplish any of this. An injury ended my competitive gymnastics career (more on this later). Excessive partying, drinking, and fighting turned me into a person I didn't know. My behavior and lack of discipline got me kicked out of college. Although I did have a lot of fun during this time, I hated the person I had become. Something had to change.

This all began to change around 2004 and 2005. I wanted to start changing some things in my life. I started to pull away from some of the people I was hanging out with. I was staying at home more. This was also around the time I got injured while working at the Chicago Park District. Since I wasn't allowed to work, at one point I decided to go visit my fraternity brother George. George was going to a junior college in Champaign, Illinois. During this trip, I decided to go to school with George. This was funny because when I was actually in school, I rarely went to class, but now I was going to a class and wasn't even in school. Well, anyway, while G. (what I usually call George) was in class, I went to the cafeteria. To make a long story short (so that I can tell the full story later), I met a friend who would introduce me to my future wife, Jillian. Meeting Jillian started a list of things that would change the rest of my life. I knew that she was different and that something special was happening.

Around this time is also when my mom (Ann, who you will hear me refer to in this book) began going to this new church. She would call me all the time, telling me that I needed to go to this new church with her. She would say that the pastor of this church was a young man and talked about the Bible in a way that I would enjoy. She would hound me every week, but I still wasn't ready yet.

Talking to a professional about these feelings and issues would have been the right thing to do. In the African American community, seeing a therapist is a sign of weakness, especially when you are a Black male. There is a saying that "if it doesn't kill you, it makes you stronger." In this case, though, what I was experiencing eventually would have killed me. You never know what will happen when your mind gets to its breaking point.

The idea to write this book actually came from my therapist. Yes, I'm a Black man who admits that he has a therapist. He felt that putting all my inner thoughts on paper would help relieve some of the pressure I put on myself. He felt it was about time that I gave myself a "pat on the back." You see, I spend so much time worrying about whether I've been able to live up to others' expectations that I never get a chance to sit back and think about all that I have done. Is this the time that I finally say to myself, "Did I make you proud?"

The chapters in this book don't have traditional chapter names. Each chapter is named after a part of a gymnastics competition. I chose to do this because gymnastics has been a great part of my life. Gymnastics has been a part of some of the happiest moments of my life and some of the saddest moments of my life. Now that I think about it, I haven't had a legitimate job in my life that didn't involve gymnastics. My life wouldn't be what it is today without gymnastics, so I chose to make it part of the story of my life.

FLOOR EXERCISE:

Where It All Began

GROWING UP, I NEVER REALLY KNEW THAT I was poor. From the pictures of myself that I see, I think I dressed pretty fly and looked pretty happy. In one picture, I have this nice, round Afro (a popular hairstyle at the time, so don't judge), this flawlessly pressed brown suit with orange accents  (thank you, 1970s), and some pretty groovy brown shoes.

I also never really knew that the neighborhood I grew up in was full of gangs and drugs either. I grew up in and around the Englewood neighborhood on the Southside of Chicago. If you watch the news these days, it seems like it's a war zone with all the shootings and murders that take place daily. From the outside looking in, people would ask me how I could live like that. I really didn't have a choice, but as crazy as it sounds, I loved this time in my life.

What I remember as a child is going with my parents to my grandfather's house almost every weekend. You see, my grandfather's house was the meetup spot for my whole family. All my aunts and uncles would be there with all their kids. We would play football in the street, tag, and a game special to my family called beer-can bowling. To play, we would take two beer cans (they didn't have to be beer cans, but since the adults started this game, they gave it this name) and put them on opposite ends of each other, maybe twenty feet apart. I would say that the setup of the game is similar to the way you set up a game of bags (cornhole). Opponents would take turns trying to roll a softball and knock over the can. If you knocked your opponent's can over, your team would get a point. I believe the winner of the game was the first team to get twenty-one points. This doesn't sound like it would be that hard, but the ground had cracks and gaps that you would have to account for when rolling the ball. This would probably explain why a lot of my family members are really good at "real" bowling. But anyway, not only did my family come to my grandfather's house, but all the neighbors were there too. We were like one big, happy family. This could be the reason why I never really felt like an only child growing up. Our families were so tight, and this was a result of what they encountered when they first moved to the neighborhood.

My mother's family was one of the first Black families to move to the neighborhood. This is hard to visualize because the news today paints a picture of gangs, drugs, and violence. The area is run-down, and all you see are black and brown faces. My Uncle Clay told me a story about this white gang called "the Burger King Boys" who would terrorize the neighborhood when they were growing up. This gang would try to catch the young Black boys alone so that they could attack and beat them up. Because of this, the Black boys would have to join together to defend each other and their area of the neighborhood. While protecting themselves and their "hood," these boys ended up forming some lifelong friendships. This is also how the two sides of my family would be forever connected.

Protecting the neighborhood is how my dad's and my mom's families met. They were almost forced to be together to survive in this environment. I guess in a way, I can give

 credit to my Uncle Clay for my parents getting together. Clay started dating my Aunt Lue (now his wife of fifty years), and my Aunt Lue was friends with my mom. Since my dad and uncle were protecting the neighborhood

together, and his girlfriend and my mom were friends, they were just destined to get together. Like my Aunt Lue tells it, it was love at first sight for my mom (who I usually just refer to as Ann). Early in their relationship, Aunt Lue says that you could always tell when my dad was off work. First off, my mom would start getting freshened up, and then you could hear the engine of my dad's (Butch is what I call him) 1974 Dodge Charger (yes, he liked fly cars). From what I was told, my grandmother used to tease my mom all the time about how she would react when hearing my dad's car hit the block. My mom and grandmother had a really good relationship, so the teasing would always get a good laugh.

My mom and dad had similar family dynamics growing up. They both came from large families. My mom had seven siblings (my uncles Robert, Clay,

Lamont, Fred, and Antonio; my Aunt Neicy and another sister, Bernice, who died at a very early age of pneumonia). My dad had eight siblings in his family (my uncles Johnny, Steve, Terry, Jerry, and Russell, and my aunts Yvonne, Sharon—a.k.a. Bett—and Nikita). I never met my mom's mother, but I only hear great things about her. She was a light-skinned woman with thin, wavy hair. She was about five feet seven with really long legs. Education was very important  to my grandmother, and graduating high school was mandatory. During the process of writing this book, I learned just how important education was to her. My Aunt Lue had a goal of going to Spelman College, but she ended up getting pregnant with my oldest cousin, Antricia (known to us in the family as Peter), and decided that staying local for college would be a better decision for her family. The problem was that Aunt Lue didn't have the twenty dollars needed to pay for the registration fee. Lue didn't have anyone to go to for the money because her family was poor, and her dad didn't feel that education was that important. Lue's dad felt that education beyond reading and writing was useless. My grandmother gave Lue (her son's then-girlfriend) the money to register for college, which may have changed the direction of Lue's future. I think my grandmother knew that if she didn't give Lue that twenty dollars, her first grandchild, Antricia, would be stuck in the cycle of poverty that consumed most of the people from the neighborhood. People say that my grandmother would give you the shirt off her back if you needed it.

My mom's dad, Albert Moore (Daddy Mo'), was also a great man. He was a very dark-skinned man with a thin frame. He was a really cool guy who liked to wear nice hats. I honestly  don't remember a time when he didn't have some type of hat on. He loved to dance, and he and my grandmother would have parties on the weekend and dance all night long. He was a hard worker who loved to spoil his kids. The only bad thing that anyone could say about him was that he had some issues with drinking. He didn't always have this problem, as he was more of a social drinker. After losing his job and not having a better way to deal with it, he turned to the bottle. Regardless of that, he was a great listener (and knew everyone's business), gave good advice, and saved me from a lot of spankings as a child.

My aunts and uncles on my mom's side were pretty athletic too. My Uncle Clay ran track, Fred played baseball and softball, and Lamont and Tonio played football. My mom didn't do organized sports, but from what I've heard, she was pretty fast and loved to play volleyball. Many of my family members tell stories of how fast she was and how she would beat all the boys in the neighborhood. This is probably where I got my athletic ability from.

Life for my mom's family drastically changed for them when her mother got sick. My mom's mother was diagnosed with lupus and passed when my mom was in her late teens. At this time, instead of hanging out with her friends and enjoying her teenage years, she now had to start taking care of the family. She had to cook for the family and make sure that her dad and her younger siblings had the things that they needed. This wasn't easy for her, but she made it work.

My dad was born in Jackson, Mississippi, in the early 1950s. He and his family moved to Chicago when he was a  young boy. His dad was around but not really there in the household. He tells me stories about how poor they were, but they didn't know that they were poor because everyone in the neighborhood was also poor. Now, on the other hand, my dad had to take on a fatherly role for his siblings, according to my Aunt Nikita.

Although my Uncle Johnny was the oldest, from what I've

been told, my dad was the most

responsible sibling. Their mom was

a single mom, so my dad stepped in

and took on the role of head of the

household. My dad's family wasn't

athletic like my mom's side of the

family. They were just trying to make do with so many

children in one household.

Although I cared for all of them, I was probably closer

to my Aunt Nikita, my Uncle Terry, my Aunt Sharon (Bett),

and my Aunt Yvonne. My Aunt Nikita was my cool aunt. She

always had nice clothes and was known for "keeping it real."

I know that I can always go to her and get her honest opinion.

Her counterpart was my Uncle Terry, my dad's youngest

sibling. He was the uncle who could always make me laugh.

He wasn't a joke teller, but his mannerism and quick

comebacks would keep you entertained. I remember when I

used to come home from college, I would always go to the Circle to hang out and have a beer with Terry. Then there was

my Aunt Bett, who in my young eyes was the rich one of the family. After high school, she got a good job with ComEd and she moved downtown. I remember for Christmas and birthday's she would always give my cousins and I cash gifts. Finally, there was my Aunt Yvonne, my dad's oldest sister. She was a no-nonsense person. She reminded me of Nell Carter from the sitcom *Gimme a Break*. She didn't play any games at all, and you knew that if she said something, she meant it. I didn't see her as a very caring person, so I was surprised to see that she had kept a framed copy of a newspaper article that featured me in her bedroom.

My parents were together awhile before they got pregnant with me. From what I was told, Ann was one of the last of her friends to get pregnant. The family was super happy when they got the news of Ann's pregnancy. It was almost like an "about time" moment for them. During the pregnancy, Ann and my Aunt Lue were pretty close. She was even with her when she was in the delivery room. My dad took my mom and Aunt Lue to the hospital, but he didn't want to be in the hospital room. Maybe because he didn't want to faint or something (ha!). But while in the delivery room, Lue said that my mom didn't want to get an epidural at first. Whenever she felt a contraction, she would pretty much throw Aunt Lue into the wall. Every time Ann threw her against the wall, she would come right back to her side. That's what you call a real friend, because after that first push into the wall, I would have had to step out of that room. Eventually, I came into the world, and my dad came into the room to hold me. What my mom remembers most about this time is how big my hands were.

After taking me home and deciding that she didn't like their living conditions, my mom made up her mind that something had to change. She now had a baby boy and didn't want to bring me up in the place where she was living. She describes the apartments as like the Carter Apartments in the movie *New Jack City*. She said that the building had a lot of apartments, and drugs were being sold everywhere. She hated living there, but that's all that she could afford.

Shortly after I was born, my mom enrolled in one of the local junior colleges and worked at the college full time. At the time, my dad worked in the construction industry as a bricklayer. So now my mom was going to school full time, working full time at the college, and taking care of me. I attended a preschool program at the junior college, and when my mom got off work, she would take me to my grandfather's house or the babysitter's house. Then she would head back to the junior college to attend class at night. She did most of this traveling back and forth on the bus because my dad would already be at work with the car.

They did this until they were finally able to get a better place on Seventy-Eighth and Marshfield in Chicago (now known as Killa Ward). I loved it in this apartment because we were all together. The building looked like a red castle to me. It had three floors, with two apartments on each floor. And of course, we lived on the third floor, meaning that I got some really strong legs walking up and down all those stairs every day. There were three bedrooms in our apartment. My parents had the big room, then there was my room toward the back of the place, and behind that was what ended up being my workout room and playroom. In the front of our apartment were a lot of windows, and in this room, my dad had a lot of different plants and a huge fifty-five-gallon fish tank. I loved to be in this room because both my dad and I have a love for fish, and I loved helping him water the plants. My mom would cook lasagna, my favorite dish at the time (although now it's her smothered chicken and gravy with rice), and my dad would play music on the record player on

Sundays as we cleaned up the apartment. He would play all kinds of music, from Al Green, to Anita Baker, to Journey. This is where I believe that I got my love for music. This is definitely when I found the love for my favorite singer of all time, Miss Anita Baker.

I remember Christmas in that apartment because we had a tree, and there were always lots of gifts. I also recall my Uncle Antonio coming over during Christmastime because he knew I would get cool things like racetracks and video games like the Texas Instrument (before Atari, I believe), and he loved to play my games and stuff. There is another story from this time that still cracks me up to this day. My mom was the disciplinarian of the house, meaning she handed out all spankings. Well, one day, I must have done something very bad because my dad was coming after me to give me the first spanking that he would ever try to give me. But I guess I didn't think this was the right day. When he started coming, I started running. Their room had two doors, so I hopped over the bed, went through the door, and he came right behind me. We kept this up until he got too tired to chase me anymore. Just say, I didn't get that spanking that day and can't remember him ever getting that mad at me again. Those were the days—the days when things just seemed so simple.

Even though we had our own place then, we would still go to my grandfather's house on Loomis on the weekends when I didn't have a gymnastics competition. Things at home were starting to change a lot though. My parents weren't getting along as well as they once were, and they ended up separating. My dad moved out, and my mother and I moved in with my grandfather on Loomis while she was trying to figure things out. Things were starting to change a little bit on Loomis too. It was the 1980s, and crack was starting to come into the inner city. You would think that I would begin to notice the violence in the area, but that's not what caught my young eye. What caught my eye were the dope boys and the things that they had. They had really flashy jewelry and cars. I remember wondering how they could get all those cool things. Eventually I would witness some of the violence when one of the dope boys was shot right on my grandfather's street. I remember this night very well. My mom and I were upstairs in our room, and we heard gunshots. It wasn't unusual to hear gunshots, but these shots were closer than usual. After the shooting stopped, I got off the floor and wanted to see what was going on. The next thing I saw was my neighbor stumbling across the street. Thankfully, he survived the shooting. Things like that happened so often in the hood that you just kind of got numb to them.

After some time, my parents still weren't getting along and ended up getting divorced. I remember after the divorce, things drastically changed for me, and I told myself I was never getting married because marriages don't last. The weird thing is that even though they were going through their thing, they made sure that I still had gymnastics. Around this time, my dad became a police officer, and my mom became a teacher. My mom and I moved to a couple more crappy places after that. One of these places was on Sixty-Second and Artesian. I was a teenager when we moved over there, and I remember not feeling safe at all. There was a dope spot right across the street, and prostitutes would also be in and out of that building. This was also a GD (Gangster Disciple) neighborhood and wasn't really safe for me because all of my friends whom I associated with were pretty active Vice Lords and Black Stones. I had to limit myself to things I could do before the streetlights came on because it wasn't safe to go out after dark.

We lived over there until my mom was finally able to buy us a house in a really good neighborhood. This house was on West Eighty-Third, a couple of blocks east of Kedzie. It was a quiet neighborhood with a park about a block away. This was a neighborhood full of firefighters and police officers, so it was really quiet. Now the house itself was a small, ranch-style house. It was a two-bedroom house with an addition at the back of the house that had a hot tub and entertainment room. I guess the previous owners used to host a lot of parties there. It wasn't a big house, but it was ours.

Growing up as an only child wasn't as bad or as boring as some would think. For selfish reasons, I liked it that way. I didn't have to share my toys…ha! Sometimes I think about what having a sibling would have done for my life at this time. Would I have still been able to do gymnastics at the level that I did? Traveling as much as I did already put a strain on the family finances. What if my sibling didn't do gymnastics and chose another sport? Would my gymnastics have interfered with what they were doing? I think things worked out the way they were supposed to. My "siblings" ended up being my cousins, teammates, and other friends. I really didn't have that much time to notice that I was alone. During the week, I was at gymnastics practice. At my most intense point, I was in the gym almost six days a week. My dad had another child when I was a little older. My sister and I aren't really that close and have never lived in the same household. I would like to get to know her a little better one day.

If I wasn't at gymnastics practice, I was on Loomis at my grandfather's house. When I was on Loomis, like I mentioned before, I had pretty much my whole family there. Most of the time, the adults were having a good time playing cards, drinking some adult beverages, or listening to the blues. We've probably heard every blues singer to ever make music. I think their favorite singer was Johnnie Taylor. I could always tell when one of his songs came on because the

card game would stop, and the singing and dancing would start. We are a very musical family on my mom's side. My Aunt Neicy would

sometimes sing Patti LaBelle, and she was so good that you would think Patti had come over to visit. My Uncle Lamont was no slouch either, and when he sang "Love Calls," by Kem, it felt like a real concert was taking place. They would battle, song for song, for hours. And then there was my "cousin sister" (as she refers to herself) Alania; when she sings, chills go up and down your spine. I love to hear her sing. She is one of the best singers that I've heard, and I would put her up against anyone.

Now my cousins and I would be running all around everywhere, but my Uncle Tonio's room and the basement are where we did the most damage—at least when we weren't running around outside. The basement was the *spot*! I had my best birthday parties ever in that basement, and if I'm not mistaken, I was also the DJ. The basement was probably the place where I also saw my first gang fight. My cousin Nookie was having a party, and her friends were there. Some other guys came through, causing problems, and that's all they needed. The fight started in the basement and then spilled out into the streets and everything. There was also a future two-time NBA champion who was at this party, but I'll keep that name to myself. Although that was the first gang-related incident that happened, it wasn't the last.

There is one event that I don't think I will ever forget. Everyone was sitting on the porch on Loomis, like they always were, and a neighbor was walking by on his way home, which was two houses away. As a car pulled on the block, an AK-47 came out from the car and began to fire down the block. I've never seen anyone move so fast. I think my grandfather beat everyone in the house after hearing the shots. No one was hit, but my Uncle Lamont's red Chevy Nova was toast. What's crazy is that after the smoke cleared, everyone was right back outside like nothing ever happened. It was just normal to us at that point.

The next event was when I was a little older. My cousins and I, along with some of the neighbors' kids, were walking to the store in Moe Town, a neighborhood where the Black Stones gang was. We would take this walk from time to time, and usually everything was fine. But this day, a girl recognized me from being with some of my friends from the Circle (the neighborhood where my dad's family lived) and yelled out, "He's a hook" (the term that they called Vice Lords, a rival gang). Before I get too deep into this story, let me explain the dynamics of inner-city neighborhoods at this time. If you lived in a neighborhood that was predominately GDs, then to everyone else outside that neighborhood, you were GD, too, and vice versa. In this next situation, this girl had probably seen me around the "Circle," which was mostly Vice Lords and Black Stones, or saw me with some of my friends who were affiliated. Now back to my story. I heard a whistle, and before I knew it, there were guys everywhere. My first instinct was to get out of there, but I had my little cousins with me, so I knew I had to stay and fight. I remember hitting one of them, and then after that, I just felt punches coming from everywhere. Right when things could have gotten worse, I saw two things. First, I saw my Uncle Tonio driving down the block, and next my cousin Nookie was running down the block with a really big knife. We had been saved! I told everyone to make sure they didn't tell my mom, because she would never let me come over there again. That secret stayed with us for a very long time. Actually, I'm not sure, but when she reads this book, it may be the first time she hears the real story. As violent as that incident was, and as much pain as I was in afterward, I still enjoyed being over there on Loomis. The situation was taken care of anyway after that, and we never had a problem out of those guys again.

There were more good memories than bad ones from my time on Loomis. Until my grandfather died, I just remember how close we all were. The times I had with all my cousins are priceless. The dancing and singing, the birthday parties, and the holiday dinners are all times that I really miss. After my grandfather died in 1993, the family just wasn't the same anymore, but I really hope, for the sake of his memory, that we can get that back.

As a youngster, I also spent a lot of time around my paternal grandmother's house in a neighborhood that we called the Circle. The Circle was a neighborhood that was kind of secluded from everywhere else. There was only really one way in and out of the neighborhood. That made it safer for us as kids because there wasn't a whole lot of traffic. In the middle, there was this grassy island where we would play football and other sports. It was like our practice facility for when we would play other outside blocks in sports. When we were younger, Baby D, P. J., Snoop, some others, and I would play tag in the Circle. We would use the whole neighborhood, running through people's yards and hopping fences to get away from whoever was "it." This would come in handy in the future when "outsiders" or the police came into the neighborhood. The Circle is where I met some of my closest friends and where I hung out with my cousins Jermaine and Re-Re. I wasn't as close to everyone on my dad's side, but I was close to them. Re-Re was a little older than me by a month or so, and Jermaine was younger by a couple years.

As I got older, I would spend more and more time in the Circle. Once my parents got divorced, that's where I would go to see my dad. He lived at my grandmother's house (I later found out he actually owned the house), and his bedroom was in the basement. The Circle was a lot safer than my maternal grandfather's house on Loomis initially, but in the mid '80s and early '90s, things began to change. This is also when crack began to creep into Black communities. I noticed some of the older guys in the neighborhood starting to dress nicer and drive nicer cars. I was intrigued by this because I was into fashion and loved cars. I could hang around them because they always wanted to know about how I was doing in gymnastics. You see, in school, my gymnastics career wasn't as popular as it was in my neighborhood. In the neighborhood, the older guys wanted me to make it to the Olympics, so they would do whatever they could do to keep me safe and away from trouble as much as they could. This made me feel good. You would think that they would be the ones making fun of me, but they were actually encouraging me to be better so that I didn't get caught up in what they were doing. Not everyone was so lucky. Some of the other guys who were around my age in the neighborhood were getting more involved in the gang activities that were starting to rise around this time. No matter how bad things were getting outside of the Circle, we were safe in our little hood.

There are only a handful of times when I got nervous in the Circle. Because of the security that people felt when being in the Circle, there would be some pretty big dice games in the Circle. One day, there was a dice game, and during the game, one of the guys drove around and alerted us of a possible stickup. Everyone broke away from the game to get to safety. I had to run down the block to get to my grandmother's house, and coming across the Circle (the grassy island), I saw a couple of guys with guns. I tried to get into the house, but no one would open the door for me. I don't know if they were scared or just didn't hear me, but no one came to open the door, so I had to get away from there as fast as I could. To get away from this, I had to run to the backyard and hop fences until I got to safety.

The next incident involved the police and is why I always had a problem with police officers growing up. I hear people say all the time, "You didn't like police officers, but your dad was a cop." My dad and his partners were normal cops. They had grown up in the "hood," so they knew how it felt to be one of us. On this particular day, Baby D. and I (who were in our early teens) were walking back from Prestige Liquors, where we had gone to get some snacks, when the cops pulled us over. The cop told his partner, "We got some hooks." This is a derogatory term they called all Vice Lords at the time. They proceeded to pull out a bag with guns in it and said, "Which one of these murders do y'all want to take?" Right when things could have gotten really ugly for us, they got another call and left us alone. I think back to how much that could have changed my life if they hadn't gotten another call.

There was also a time when I almost got killed. I was hanging out with Koolaid, Baby D., and Snoop. Koolaid was about to drive us to "the Nine," a.k.a. Seventy-Ninth Street, where Prestige Liquors was located. On the way there, we drove past a group of guys who were visiting some people in the neighborhood. As we were driving by, they pointed at me in the car, but we kept driving. I turned around and noticed they were now following us. We bent a few corners, and Koolaid got spooked, so he turned back in toward the Circle. He stopped at the stop sign on Seventy-Sixth and Hoyne. When he stopped, the guys jumped out of the car behind us and surrounded us with guns. I happened to recognize one of the guys and began to shout, "Hey, it's me, man!" He ordered everyone to put down their guns and let us go. We pulled away, and when we got to Koolaid's house, we ran and hid in the backyard.

The last incident was the one that changed everything for me. I was home from college and was in the Circle at Ahmand's (one of my best friends today) hanging out. There was a knock at the door, and as I got to the door to answer it, I saw that it was Baby D. I hadn't seen him in forever, so I went outside and gave my guy a hug, and we started to catch up. I told him that the next morning, I was going to pick him up and take him to breakfast to see what he had going on. After Baby D. left, I ended up taking my cousin Jermaine and Ahmand to Jermaine's house to chill for a minute. As soon as we got there, I got a phone call that shook my world.

I can't remember who called, but the next words I heard were "Baby D. just got shot!" We hopped in the car and raced back over to the Circle. It was true. As we pulled up, the cops were there, people were crying, and Baby D. was dead. He had been forced to lie on the ground and was shot in the back with a shotgun. It happened right in the place where we used to play sports as kids, in a place that we thought was "safe." To this day, Baby D. was the first and only person to get killed in the Circle. This kind of thing had happened around the Circle all the time, but never inside. This, in my opinion, changed the Circle forever.

As the older guys got more involved in the streets, they began to move away from the Circle to more lucrative areas. A lot of the people I knew and hung out with moved out of the state. I started hanging out more with my cousin Jermaine and some of his friends who were a little younger than me but definitely a safer crowd to be with. I also felt like I was the big brother who could keep them safe. I really got close to Ahmand, and our friendship is close to this day. No matter where I go and what I do, I am still and forever

will be a Circle Boy. Shout out to Jermaine, Ahmand, Nick, Mike, Dre, K. K., and Man-Man.

Today, I am a father to Olivia, a husband to Jillian, a son to Ann and Butch, and a stepson to Bubba. I'm a co-owner of Prairie Gymnastics Club, the Windy City Invitational, and a real estate investment company with my dad. I'm a spiritual person but not overly religious. Someone who loves to travel and hang out with family and friends and loves to laugh. Someone who loves music (not country music, though) and loves watching sports, but also likes to read. I would like to say that I am a very loyal person who hates to let people down. Where I am today came with a lot of sacrifices and sometimes pain and heartbreak, but I wouldn't trade it for anything. The things that I went through growing up prepared me for what was to come.

POMMEL HORSE:

The Life of a Black Gymnast

G YMNASTICS? A QUESTION THAT I'M ASKED a lot is "how the hell did you get into gymnastics?"

If you look at me now, you could probably see defensive lineman. But gymnast? My mom tells the story of her putting me in gymnastics so that I didn't flip off the

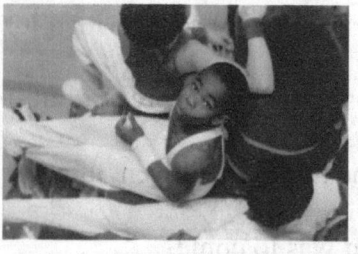 couch and hurt myself. From what I hear, there wasn't a piece of furniture that I wouldn't flip off. To keep me

safe and out of the emergency room, she went on a mission

to find a place where I could get out some of my reckless energy. The only place that she could think of that could help me safely learn how to "flip" was a gymnastics gym. The problem was that my parents didn't know a lot about gymnastics. There wasn't a Simone Biles at that time to look up to. In the inner city of Chicago at that time, the sports that young Black boys gravitated to were baseball, football, and basketball. Gymnastics was a "sport for girls," so most boys didn't really want to be involved in it. This ended up causing some problems for me in the future.

The Yellow Pages were where my mom was eventually able to find a place for me to begin my gymnastics journey. For the millennials, before you could use Google or ask Siri to help you find something, you had to look in this thick yellow book with phone numbers in it (mind blown)! Lynn Allen's gymnastics was the place where my official gymnastics career began. Lynn's gym was in the hood (a pretty bad area in an urban community), on Seventy-Fourth and Cottage Grove on the Southeast side of Chicago. My mom says that they almost turned around when they saw the building that the gym was in because it looked a little sketchy. The building was run down, but when my mom went upstairs and saw the Black lady with a tiny Afro (which she still has to this day), she knew that this was the place for me. It was not a big place at all, and I remember it being on the second floor. I don't remember a whole lot about this time because I was three years old, but I do know that I had fun. In the early stages, I remember that the skills I was learning came really easily to me, while others in the group would struggle. I did gymnastics at Lynn Allen's gym for about two years.

After that, I remember my parents telling me that I had to go to another gym. I was really upset that I had to leave my coach, because if you know me, you know that I don't deal with change very well. I didn't understand why Lynn couldn't coach me. She had other high-level kids in the gym.

One in particular was the reason I wanted to be a competitive gymnast. Although I can't remember her name now, she was the best gymnast in the world in my young eyes. She would flip on the bars like no one could. And if Lynn could coach her to do all of that, why couldn't she teach me to do the same? From what I was told, I had reached the limit of what Lynn could give me as a coach in boys' gymnastics. At that time, I didn't know there was a difference between boys' and girls' gymnastics. I didn't know that the girls had four events and the boys had six events. You see, all this time, I was only using the equipment that Lynn had, and it was mostly for girls' events. The girls' events are the uneven bars, balance beam, floor exercise, and vault (which boys and girls did).

Lynn saw that I had the potential to go really far in gymnastics and wanted me to go somewhere that could help me reach my potential. She referred me to a University of Illinois Chicago (UIC) alum who was starting to coach at Beverly Gymnastics Center, a new gym on Ninety-Ninth and

Western Avenue (the far Southside of Chicago). The gym was a lot bigger than my previous gym. If I remember correctly, it was in an old church, and the gymnastics equipment was all on the third floor. There was a lot more gymnastics equipment at this gym. Not only did I see all of the girls' equipment that I was accustomed to seeing, but there was also boys' equipment at the gym. This is where I met my new coach, George  Martenia. To the five- and six-year-old me, George was the coolest guy ever. He was a slender but athletic guy with an earring and a low haircut with a shag at the back. For those who may not know, a shag was the cool style for African American males in the '80s. It was really just a patch of hair left at the lower back of the head, but for some reason that was the coolest thing ever to me. George could also still do gymnastics. He would tumble from time to time around the gym.

My competitive career didn't start off with a bang. It wasn't a gymnastics issue per se; it was the uniform. I had to wear what looked like a leotard, some small shorts, and tight white pants. How the hell could I explain this getup to the guys in school or in my neighborhood? That was a hell of a dilemma for a six-year-old to deal with. After some convincing, I was able to move past it (kind of) and went on to have a successful first season in gymnastics. I remember my first competition at Gainers Gymnastics. Gainers Gymnastics was a club run by a Black couple named John and Judy Redmond. This experience set me up for disappointment in a way. You see, Gainers was primarily a club full of Black gymnasts. Not only were they Black gymnasts, but they were also really good. The reason that I say it was a disappointment is because I thought there were a lot of Black gymnasts in gymnastics. Boy, was I wrong.

After that competition, I got to see what the real gymnastics world looked like, and it was very white. I remember going to competitions that first year and wondering if I was that bad or if the judges just did not like me. At one point, I remember my mom having a conversation with me, telling me that I would have to be better than everyone else because of the color of my skin. I believe the sentence that she used was that the judges would take "black points." Black points are the points that are taken off when you don't look like everyone else in the competition. It used to really upset me when I knew that I was better than most of the people at the competition, and sometimes my scores just wouldn't reflect that. You may say, "How do you know that this was happening?" It was often obvious when it was happening, and just about everyone noticed, but I took what my mom said to heart. Because I'm so competitive, I made sure that they couldn't take those black points away from me anymore. From that point on, I was on a mission to be the best. By the end of that season, I placed second overall at the United States Gymnastics Federation (USGF) Illinois State Championships and was the Class 4 vault state champion.

That year, I also remember being invited to do a demonstration at the 1985 Chicago Auto Show. At this time, Nissan was a sponsor for USGF, and they picked some local gymnasts to perform with some Olympic athletes. This was a big deal to me. I was able to perform in front of the thousands of Auto Show attendees and meet some pretty cool athletes. There was one gymnast in particular named Ron Galimore whom I was so happy to meet. Ron had qualified for the 1980 Olympic Games but didn't get to compete due to the Olympic boycott. Ron was Black, and that was what was so impressive to me.

The next year, George had a disagreement with the owner of Beverly Gymnastics Center and left to coach at another gym. I was heartbroken again because I had lost another coach. I stayed at Beverly for a while after that with my new coaches: Marco Bravo and Jose Vilchis. Marco was good, but I didn't click well with Jose. I developed a fear of trampoline due to Jose purposely dropping me on my head because I bent my knees on a skill called a layout (a skill performed with a completely straight body). This situation was not going to work, and eventually we found out where George was coaching and followed him to Spartans Gymnastics in Justice, Illinois.

Spartans Gymnastics was, as I remember, a pretty small gym owned by this lady named Carol. I remember Carol being a female bodybuilder or something like that. All I truly cared about was being with George again. That year, I was training as a Class 3 gymnast. I was too young to be a Class 3 gymnast because the primary age group was nine to twelve years old, and at this time, I was only eight. There was a rule at that time in USGF that an athlete could only compete one year ahead of their actual age (or at least that's what George told me), so I was still able to compete. Class 3 was the first optional level in gymnastics. The first year I competed, I was a compulsory gymnast, meaning that I did all the same routines that everyone else in that level did. Once I made it to Class 3, I was able to have my own routines that were constructed by George. USGF gave you a few requirements that you had to have in each routine, but you could fulfill those requirements with whatever skills you had.

That first year in Class 3 was another successful year. I was state champion in my age group and had qualified for the Region 5 Championships in Michigan. The trip to  regionals was an eye-opener for me. There were so many good gymnasts there. I thought I was hot stuff after winning state championships, but I was introduced to two gymnasts who would change everything for me. At this competition, I saw Drew Durbin and Blaine Wilson (a future Olympian) doing skills I had never seen before. At that time, Drew was a better gymnast, but there was just something about Blaine. After seeing them in warm-ups, I remember being so intimidated that I pretty much blew that competition. Just say that it was not my best performance that season.

That summer I remember participating in some parades and things like that, but what I don't remember  doing is a lot of training. That next season was a blur to me, but I know that I didn't do well. The following year I switched gyms again and went to Gym-Kinetics in Glenwood, Illinois. Gym-Kinetics was not like any gym I had gone to before. This gym was huge. It had a whole area for the boys' equipment, an area for the girls' equipment, a weight room, and basketball courts. It also had something that most gyms didn't have at the time: *air-conditioning.*

Again, I had to get used to new coaches. My new coaches were the owners of the gym, Jim Frederickson and Matt Damore. Matt was my main coach and had the reputation of being pretty wild. Matt was a former UIC gymnast just like George and had been on the 1978 NCAA championship team. There was not a party that Matt didn't like, but as far as coaching goes, to me he was great. I remember after Friday night practices, I would see small boxes going into the coaches' offices. It wasn't until I got older that I realized what was in those small boxes—beer for their weekly coaches' parties. Matt would also have frequent parties at his home.

There were also visitors at Gym-Kinetics all the time. I remember a lot of former Olympic gymnasts showing up at the gym to help us and to attend those parties in the back office, which was a huge thing at that time. While training at Gym-Kinetics, I got really good, really fast. Matt had a "go chuck it" coaching style, which was perfect for my personality. In terms of training, this was the best place for me to be, but there were some issues. You see, Gym-Kinetics was about an hour away from home, and because my mom was getting into her career as an educator, she wasn't always able to get me to practice herself. So in stepped my Uncle Antonio and his best friend, Vick. For pretty much my whole time at Gym-Kinetics, Antonio and Vick would take the trip from Fifty-Seventh and Loomis in Chicago to 197th and Glenwood Dyer Road in Glenwood, Illinois, five or six days a week. I was never able to tell them how much I appreciated what they did for me. They sacrificed a large portion of their day to make sure that I was able to train in a sport that they knew very little about, but they knew how much I loved the sport.

The next thing about Gym-Kinetics was not so great. I had to deal with racism a lot more during this time, both inside and outside the gym. I didn't feel this as much from the coaches, but there were a few teammates I didn't feel as comfortable with. It wasn't all of them, but enough for me to wish that I had more teammates who looked like me and I could relate to. There were a couple of teammates who would tell racist jokes, and I even had one younger teammate tell me that he didn't like Black people. I don't even know if they realized what they were doing because we were all so young. At the age that we were, it came so naturally to them that it had to just be things that they heard at home. I knew that they didn't really mean it, but it was still very hard to deal with.

Outside the gym, it was a little tougher to deal with. While I was at a camp at the Olympic Training Center, another gymnast made it clear that I was different. When you were a member of the Junior National Developmental Team, you would have to attend camps throughout the year. At the Olympic Training Center, I was given two other roommates. Both these roommates were from Illinois, so I knew them from other competitions that we were in together. When I saw their names listed as my roommates, I thought that I would be OK. After practice we stopped by the gift shop just to look around. While in the gift shop, I wanted to pick something out for my mother, but I realized that I left my money in my room. One of my roommates did have some money with him, so I asked if I could borrow the money until I got back to the room, but he wouldn't do it because he didn't like brown people. Those were the kinds of things that I would deal with from time to time. It sucked, but that's just how things were back then, so I learned to deal with it. Things did get better at Gym-Kinetics though. My now-best-friend Scotty Blackful joined the team, and so did Maurice Black. It felt so good to have someone who looked like me at the gym. Don't get me wrong: I had always enjoyed being at Gym-Kinetics; it was just a different time in the sport of gymnastics.

With Scotty and Maurice on the team, things were a lot more fun. I had known of Scotty for a while. He was a light-skinned guy who came from the gym that I once attended (Beverly Gymnastics Center). He was a really good gymnast who was also from the Southside of Chicago. We had very similar situations, as he also lived with his mom and was the only child in the household. His mom also had to find ways to make sure he got to practice because of her work schedule. Scotty and I connected quickly and spent quite a bit of time together inside and outside of the gym. Maurice was older than us, but he was from the suburbs. Maurice was the cooler older brother that we kind of looked up to, but I remember him always getting into it with the coaches. Maurice was really cool; he had the newest haircuts, dressed really cool, and listened to hip-hop (which was pretty new at that time).

I remember his love for hip-hop got him in trouble at the gym a lot. On one occasion, while listening to some rap music, Jim (one of our coaches) came out, opened up the tape deck, and looked at the tape that Maurice had put in there. He then threw it against the wall, sending plastic pieces all over the place. Maurice didn't take this lightly, approached Jim, and ended up getting pushed into the wall. Scotty and I thought that this was the funniest thing ever, and to me, this made Maurice even cooler.

After some time, we ended up getting more Black athletes on the team. There were little Kevin (I can't remember his last name) and Na'im, and then I remember Rodell and Nate Knight joining the team. I had previously known Na'im. Na'im was on Gainers team, which was the all-Black team that I mentioned earlier. Now Ro and Nate Knight were an interesting story. While our parents were talking in the gym lobby one day, they realized that their family was from the same part of Mississippi (Jackson) that my dad was from. From that day on, we were cousins. Our "family" relationship would spill over into the rest of the gymnastics world, which was pretty funny to us. I did have some really good friends on that team who weren't Black.

There were Bill Kroshell (I don't know if that is the correct spelling of his name), John and Bob Carlson, Kevin Koperski, Nick Becker, and Brad Panazzo.

What I do remember the most about my last few years at Gym-Kinetics was being at Nationals with Scotty and Maurice. It was funny because we were the only Black kids on the team, and we were the only ones who qualified for nationals at that time. Nationals that year were in Anaheim, California. This was a great time for me because I had placed in the top five (I think third place) at the Region 5 Championships and had made the regional team again. A funny (but maybe not so funny) story about nationals in Anaheim: Matt took us (Maurice, Scotty, and myself) to an Anaheim Angels baseball game. It was minibat-giveaway night at the ballpark. So now you had three teenagers and one adult kid with minibats and bags of peanuts. I remember us playing baseball with the peanuts and seeing how many people we could hit. Then there was the ride home, when

Maurice turned the radio station (from the back seat of the rented minivan), and Matt turned around and was playfully trying to hit him to get him to switch from the rap station he found. Now remember, while Matt was playfully trying to hit him, he was also supposed to be driving the minivan. As far as the competition goes, it was almost a total disaster for me. I had just come off one of the best competitions of my life (regionals) to go to one of the worst (nationals). I completely bombed the compulsory competition, and by the end, I believe I was in 121st place (my worst showing as a competitive athlete). The only bright spot was that a couple of my scores counted toward the regional team score, and Region 5 came in third place!

The next season, Ted Haynes joined the coaching staff because Matt wasn't going to be involved as much. Ted was from Iowa State, and I remember thinking that he looked just like Michael J. Fox. He was also still a really good tumbler and vaulter. From time to time, he would randomly throw really cool tumbling passes. If we couldn't figure out a vault, he would just show us how it was done. We gave Ted the hardest time at the beginning. I remember us trying to get him fired at one point, because he "didn't know what he was doing." He was actually a great coach, teaching us better technique than we got from Matt.

Scotty and I had another good season the following year. Maurice had graduated and moved on to gymnastics at UIC. Scotty and I qualified for National Championships again that season in Austin, Texas. I had a better competition, and it was a lot tamer this time traveling with Ted. The following season, Scotty quit gymnastics because the injuries were starting to be a little too much.

The year was now 1993, and I was training with Matt, who was being consulted by C. J. Johnson, who was the head coach at UIC. Matt's plan was for me to take a break from USGF (United States Gymnastics Federation) competition and focus on training for the Olympics, which would be in

Atlanta in 1996. So instead of USGF, we decided to compete in the Illinois High School Association (IHSA) Series through Whitney M. Young Magnet High School. C. J. Johnson helped Matt figure out what requirements were needed in IHSA gymnastics. Since C. J. was Matt's collegiate coach, he also gave him other coaching advice and helped Matt get me registered as a high school athlete. Initially, Whitney Young was not very supportive of my idea to compete as an individual gymnast representing their school. To compete as an individual, I needed authorization from the school, along with a sponsor (a faculty member) to attend all the competitions with me.

After struggling to get the thumbs-up from the school, we finally got it, but we would have to pay for the sponsor to attend the competitions because the school wouldn't do it. Although the school wasn't supportive initially, my sponsor, Maryanne Stojak, was extremely excited. With her now on board, I felt things would be a lot better. The only difficult part was that I would have to train twice as hard. I had to work on Olympic compulsory routines as well as my high school routines. We made all my high school routines easier so that I wouldn't put as much stress on my body. There were some things going on at that time with me mentally, but I'll discuss that a little later. Back to starting my first-ever high school season: I recall going to my first competition and being shocked by the equipment that they competed on. Some of the equipment was old, and the floor exercise was a sixty-foot tumbling strip covered by a wrestling mat. That took some getting used to, but the part that I really enjoyed was the high school gymnastics atmosphere. There was so much energy in the gym. Everyone was cheering for their

teammates very loudly, unlike the super quiet and intense USGF environment. Although I was competing as an individual, the

other teams would pull me into whatever group I was

rotating with and treat me as if I were also their teammate. The first competition went really well, except for the questionable score that I received on still rings. The reason I say it was questionable was because I had the highest start value of anyone at the competition but got one of the lowest scores. Matt and I got a laugh out of that and just said maybe the judge wasn't up to date on the value of the skills that I was doing as a sophomore competing in the varsity division.

Throughout the season, things got better and better for me, but there was a small problem. You see, what I didn't tell anyone was that at practice earlier in the season, I had dislocated my left shoulder. I knew it was dislocated because I felt it pop out, and as I hit the floor, I felt it pop back in. I didn't want to tell anyone about it because that meant that I would have to end my season, and I didn't want to let anyone down. I competed the whole season with the injury, taking ibuprofen for the pain and icing the injury as much as possible.

My performance as a sophomore in 1993 got me noticed by the Chicago media. During the season, it felt like I was doing weekly interviews with the *Chicago Sun-Times* and *Chicago Tribune*. This made me very popular at school and in the high school gymnastics community. Leading up to the IHSA State Series, I was ranked second to senior Jon Wasik. After I qualified for state, there were articles written about me having a chance to win. Once at state, I had a very good meet and ended placing second in the All-Around Competition and qualified for five out of six events for event finals. In high school, gymnasts competed two events at a time in finals. The first two were the floor exercise and pommel horse. My first event was pommels, and I hit a pretty good set, but there was a lot of discussion after my routine by the judges. After what seemed like a ten-minute discussion, I was given a score of 9.3, which turned out to be .05 lower than the pommel horse champion, senior Ryan

Trent. A judge who was on that panel recently told me that he thought I should have won that event.

Next up, I had floor exercise. I started with a double full (a flip that has two twists before you land), followed by some flair spindles (skills taken from the pommel horse), then I did a handspring layout front. My next pass was a skill that has now been banned called a Marinitch. This skill started like a handspring, but you pushed off your hands and missed your feet, landing back on your hands and rolling out. If done incorrectly, you could end up with a severe neck or head injury. I finished my last pass and stuck the landing, and the gym went crazy. I was named 1993 Floor Exercise State champion. I placed really well on other events, but that was the highlight of the competition for me.

After that competition, my shoulder was killing me, but I still kept it to myself as much as I could. I had one more competition to compete in. I had promised some friends that I would compete in the Beach Meet hosted by the Chicago

Park District. This was a fun competition that actually took place on the beach. We had so much fun at this competition, but in event finals while doing pommel horse, I felt something pop. After the pop, I noticed that I had limited use of my arm. I immediately went to my mom, who was sitting in the bleachers, and let her know that something was wrong. After I went to the doctor, he revealed that I had a torn rotator cuff, and he couldn't initially find the long head of the bicep tendon. To repair it, I would have to have another surgery to fix everything that was going wrong in there. The problem with this surgery was that I would lose a lot of the range of motion in my shoulder, which would end my career as a gymnast competing in all six events. For most people, this would be devastating, but I was dealing with a lot of mental issues at the time.

Although the high school season was fun, I actually hated gymnastics. I was burned out and was only doing gymnastics because everyone had expectations of me. So in my brain, the injury was the best thing that could have happened to me. It meant that I didn't have to compete anymore, and I could be a regular high school kid. I decided that I wanted to play high school football. Football was fun for me. People may not believe me, but in a way, it was easier than gymnastics for me. Yes, there was way more contact, but football practices were shorter than gymnastics practices. There was an offseason, which I loved. During my time in gymnastics, I don't ever remember being off except for a week here or there. This was more of a team sport too. I really had to depend on my teammates if we were going to win. The bond that I had with my football teammates was closer than almost any of my gymnastics teammates. Football also allowed me to take out my aggression on the rival teams, and it was encouraged. Football allowed me to hang out more with friends and have a lot more idle time, which wasn't the best situation for me. I had more time to

hang out with the guys from the neighborhood and began to
get in a little more trouble.

RINGS:
My Educational Journey

MOST PEOPLE REPRESENT WHAT COLLEGE they went to, but for me, I am prouder of my high school. I attended Whitney M. Young Magnet High School. The high school of Joan Higginbotham (astronaut), Russell Maryland (NFL football player), Katrina Adams (tennis player), and of course Michelle Obama (our first African American First Lady). I didn't always want to go to Whitney Young though. I wanted to attend Chicago Vocational High School (CVS), where my cousin Nookie (Trinu Moore) went. I also wanted to attend Simeon Vocational High School, where my Uncle Lamont went. My mom vetoed both of those choices right away. Since my mom was an educator, she wanted me to attend the best school in Chicago, which at the time (*and, in my opinion, still is*) was one of the top schools in Illinois, if not the country.

Let me back up a little bit so you can get a little more insight on why Whitney Young was where my mom wanted me to go. I went to kindergarten at Clara Barton Elementary School, which was just the neighborhood school when we lived on Seventy-Eighth and Marshfield. There was nothing special about this school at all. According to my mom, the teachers wanted me to skip first grade because I was more advanced in every subject than all the kids in my grade. I don't know if I was that much smarter than the other kids or if my mom just spent more time teaching me things than most parents at that time. I remember her going over vocabulary words and math problems. I used to have nightmares as a kid, and to help me not be so afraid, she would turn my nightmares into funny books. That was the only thing that helped me get through that tough time.

The nightmares started around the time my Uncle Robert was murdered. It was a really hard time for my family and me, but those books helped me get through it. My mom didn't allow me to skip first grade and instead took me out of that school. For first grade, I ended up at Beasley Academic Center. Beasley Academic Center was a magnet school, one of the top elementary schools in Illinois at the time. Beasley was a beautiful new school compared to the old building that housed my last school. The only bad thing about Beasley was that it was right across the street from the projects. You had one of the top schools in the state right across the street from one of the most dangerous housing projects in the area. The majority of the students didn't even live in the area, so we were bussed in from all across the city.

Now let me describe this school to the best of my ability. The side of the building that faced the projects (where we entered the building and all the buses parked) was off-white concrete without any windows. It was like they didn't want the people who lived in the projects to see what was going on. The back of the building had the area where we would go out to play. It had lots of grass and other concrete structures for us to sit on. Inside, most people don't believe me, but we had four cafeterias. We had a decent-sized auditorium, foreign language rooms, and a wood shop. The next thing that school had—and no one ever believes me when I tell them this—was a full-sized indoor swimming pool. My mom definitely approved of this school. We had to take a foreign language starting in first grade. I don't know how I chose my first foreign language, but mine was French. I took French for six years, and today I only remember how to count to ten.

Academically, that first year was great, but mentally, it was not so good. You see, when I came back for second grade, I found out that my best friend, Bernard, had been killed by a car while walking to a gas station after his dad's car ran out of gas. That was my first friend who died violently, but it wasn't the last. The rest of my years at

Beasley went off without a hitch. I got a very good education from Beasley, and it prepared me for my next school, Whitney M. Young Magnet High School. For most of the people graduating from Beasley, Whitney Young was their first choice. Whitney Young was not easy to get into. Back in the day, after you applied, you had to get accepted, and after you got accepted, you still had to take an entrance exam. I ended up passing that exam with flying colors. I tested into honors English as well as a couple of other classes.

I still remember my first day of high school. I remember hoping that the upperclassmen wouldn't throw any pennies at me. (Throwing pennies at freshmen was a big thing back then.) Anyway, I walked into the building and went on a mission to find my first class. I was lost but definitely trying to act like I didn't need any help from anyone. I finally found my first class; it was honors English, I believe. I sat down, trying to act like I was supercool and confident (even though I was nervous). The teacher began talking and, at some point, gave us the assignment of interviewing one of our classmates. This is when I met a friend who I'm still happy to call a friend to this day. Her name is Latrice Smith (Davis). She was the first person at the school to know about my gymnastics career. What was nice about it was I remember her being really interested in my story. I was really happy because she didn't judge me negatively because I was a Black boy who did gymnastics. She was a true friend. We stayed close throughout high school and recently connected again after years of lost contact.

The first year of high school was mixed for me. Some of my other friends in my neighborhood had started getting in street activities. They never really wanted me to get involved with them, but it was just so interesting to me. They were tough, and they were making money, but I knew my parents would kill me if I got involved. There was this other thing that also kept me from getting involved: gymnastics. At this time, I was training a lot. I was in the gym somewhere between twenty and thirty hours a week. As I moved into my sophomore year, Chicago was getting more violent (the murder rate was well into the 900s in 1992 and 1993), and my friends were getting deeper into the street life. I remember seeing a lot of shootings and attending even more funerals. Even with gymnastics, it was kind of hard to keep a distance from the street activities. I was still training, but I was being heavily influenced by the streets. Around this time, you almost had to be affiliated with something just to survive. Even if you didn't want to be, depending on the neighborhood you lived in, people associated you with that gang anyway.

At this time, the worst thing you could be was a neutron (not affiliated with any gang). For example, one day

I had to ride the bus home from school for some reason. I had to take the number 9 (Ashland bus) to Seventy-Ninth Street and then the Seventy-Ninth Street bus to Albany and walk over to Eighty-Third Street, where I lived. Now let me describe this trip. As we got on the bus, some folks (Gangster Disciples) were on the bus messing with people. Now I have on a red-and-black coat (Black Stone colors, but they just happen to be my favorite colors), and one of my friends may have had his hat tilted slightly to the left. These guys were trying to make him take his hat off, but I told him not to. Now the reason I told him not to wasn't because I'm a hard-core gangster. It was mostly because if he took off the hat, we would guarantee that they would try to punk us anyway. This confrontation lasted almost until we made it to Seventy-Ninth Street.

When we got off on Seventy-Ninth Street, these same guys got off at the same stop. I was super nervous because this was the rival neighborhood, where all my friends were, and I had definitely been seen with them. So I was waiting for the bus, which I saw off in the distance, and I also saw that these guys had gotten some of their friends and were heading back to the bus stop. The bus got there right before the guys made it to me, and I remember pleading with that bus driver to not open the door for them. I survived that incident, but it wasn't the last one that I would have. That was also the last time that I rode the number 9 bus.

There were other things going on at this time in my immediate family. My mom met a new guy. Up to this point, it had just been her and me. She had just started earning enough money to buy a house for us, and I had gotten used to it just being us. And now here comes Bubba. Bubba was a cowboy—a real-life cowboy. He was a competitive calf roper with the Black Cowboys. He was super tall and drove a really nice car. I remember being cool with this until he moved in. I wasn't used to another man being in the house since Butch (my dad) moved out. Once he moved in, things began to change, and there was a new man of the house. Like any other teenage boy, I had a problem with that. We butted heads from time to time, but he wasn't a horrible dude. Although we didn't get along the best all the time, I was able to learn some things from him, just watching how he moved. Bubba knew a whole lot of people, and I would watch how he moved when he was in certain circles and how he demanded attention. He would also give me advice sometimes about just surviving in the streets. He probably didn't think that I was listening, but, Bubba, I was listening.

By this time, since I wasn't doing gymnastics anymore, I had a lot more free time on my hands, and I was spending more time with my friends. I know that Bubba saw this and would  make comments from time to time to let me know to keep my nose clean. At this time, I was not in a good place mentally. One of my good friends had committed suicide, I wasn't doing gymnastics anymore, and my parents were divorced. I was getting a little more short-tempered and had some violent moments. There were two incidents that happened my senior year in high school. One occurred when I was driving my mom and my friend to school. I think my mom and I were having some kind of disagreement, and this lady behind me started blowing her horn because I guess I wasn't moving fast enough after the light turned green. If anyone really knows me, they know that I hate for someone to blow their horn at me. It sent me into a rage that at the time I didn't know how to control. I remember getting out of the car, yelling, and acting a damn fool. Knowing myself at that time, I would have tried to pull her out of the car, had Ann not stopped me.

The next incident happened at school. There was a little situation in which my friend and another boy were getting into a confrontation by my locker area. I went over to stop the altercation, but suddenly, I felt a sharp pain in my eye. This kid had punched me in the face. I snapped, and—without going into too much detail—an ambulance was called for the kid, and I ended up with a disorderly conduct charge (I was still a minor). I was suspended from school for ten days and suspended for one football game. After that incident, I was forced to go to some anger management classes because I was completely out of control.

Around this time, my good friend since my Beasley days committed suicide over a girl. I remember this day so clearly. I was walking up the stairs going to the lunchroom in Gold House (it was called Gold House because all the chairs in the lunchroom were gold) and saw everyone crying. I mean, even the guys on the football team who I know were tough guys were overcome with emotion. When I could finally get someone to put some words together without sobbing, I was told the devastating news. My friend, whom I had known for so long, had ended his life over a breakup with a girl. I lost it. This kid and I had been friends since first grade! This was another blow to my mental state. The school arranged for me and a few of the guys who were closest to him to see a school counselor once a week for the rest of the school year. The rest of my high school years went well for the most part. I graduated and went off to college at Southern Illinois University in Carbondale (SIU).

I never really wanted to go to college. I have no clue what my plan was, but college wasn't part of it. For my mother's sake, I applied to one school, and that school was SIU. I knew that my good friend at the time was going, so I figured I might as well go there. I had heard through the grapevine that SIU was a party school, so I thought at least I would have some fun. And let me tell you, it did not disappoint. The very first night, there was a party at the recreation center. This party was nuts, and right away I realized that I was going to enjoy this college thing. I also realized that more people I knew from Whitney Young were also attending SIU. At this first party, I saw my boy Hootie

Mac, Cotto, Sabrina, Derrick, and a few others I can't remember. I had some partners in crime to help me enjoy this new college experience.

SIU was a different environment, though, and it took some time getting used to. First, the school was very divided. Everyone for the most part hung with their own race. Most of the Black and Hispanic kids were in the Towers (the three high-rise buildings on campus). The majority of the white and Asian kids were in Thompson Point (the nicer housing). There were a few that they would mix into each of the areas, but for the most part, that's how it was. Racial tensions were pretty high, and at one point, they exploded. It was around the time of the O. J. Simpson trial. I remember toward the end of the trial, one of the skinheads on campus had put a sign in his window that read, "FRY OJ." At this time, no one in the Black community wanted to hear anything like that, so we politely went to his room and asked him if he could please change that sign (I'm totally being sarcastic here). He changed the sign, but he wasn't that happy about it.

At SIU, if you wanted to do well, you had to be really focused. Let me tell you how this school was set up. I lived in Scheider Hall, which was one of the farthest dorms from campus. To get to one of my first classes, I would have to walk through the student center. Now this is why there was an issue. In the student center was the pool hall (where everyone would hang out), the bowling alley (where everyone would hang out), and McDonald's (you guessed it—where everyone would hang out). And if you made it past all those distractions, you had to walk almost a mile through the damn woods to get to some of your classes. I didn't make it past the distractions. As a matter of fact, I dove headfirst into the distractions. I found out why they called SIU a party school and didn't miss an opportunity to keep that reputation alive. I did go to the classes that I enjoyed; I didn't miss any class that had something to do with business. Economics, both micro and macro, were my favorite classes, but I may have missed a few finite math and introduction to art classes.

In my second semester, some of the guys and I saw a flyer for a party off campus hosted by a guy named Sugar Bear. We had never heard of him, but, hey, it was a party with free liquor, so we were going. It turned out to be one of the best parties that we had gone to since making it to Carbondale. We ended up talking to Sugar Bear, and he told us about this new Black Greek-lettered organization that he was part of. It was called Beta Phi Pi Incorporated. It was founded in 1986 at Western Illinois University, and Sugar Bear (Kevin) was trying to start a chapter at SIU. I was *wilding* out at the time, so I thought this might add a little structure to my college experience, and it did while I was pledging. We did all the stupid stuff that you think goes on while pledging. I was going to class—we had library and gym hours—so there was some structure. My temper did get me in a little trouble from time to time, and we did almost beat up one of the big brothers, but in the end, we all became brothers.

After becoming one of the bros, I felt what college life was really about. I found out what being in a frat was really like. Since we were a new Black Greek-lettered organization on campus, the older frats didn't give us a lot of respect. This is where my violent tendencies began to show their faces again. I began being known for being good with my hands. That was one good thing about being on a college campus; people would still fight and not shoot. Fraternity life wasn't all about partying and fighting. I met a group of men with whom I have created some lifelong bonds. The fraternity brothers that I have met created a network base that stretches across many valuable industries. These connections have helped me do a lot of things that make my businesses successful today.

After two years at SIU, I was told that my attendance at the university was no longer necessary. The way that I found out that I was kicked out of the school is funny now, but it definitely was not funny at the time. I had a disciplinary hearing for a fight I had gotten into, and they notified me that I would be suspended from the school. They mailed a letter to my house, but when the letter arrived, I got to the mailbox first and removed it. My plan was to go back to the SIU campus when school started and attend classes at the junior college until I could get back into SIU. What I didn't know was that SIU had sent a second letter, and I didn't catch that one, but Ann did. While I was hanging out with the guys in the Circle, I received a call from Ann, and she stated that I needed to come home right away. When I got home, she had the letter sitting out, and I instantly knew that it was going to be a long day. It was definitely not one of my better moments and not a situation that I am very proud of.

VAULT:
Coaching for a Purpose

I WOULD LIKE TO START THIS CHAPTER BY saying I never wanted to be a gymnastics coach. I only started coaching for financial reasons. I was able to do very little work but got paid more than any of my friends. My coaching career started in high school.

George, my first competitive coach, was working for the Chicago Park District at Garfield Park on the Westside of Chicago. This was a pretty rough side of town. He needed a little help with his growing team, so I got hired and became his assistant coach. At this time, I wasn't training as much at Gym-Kinetics, so on days when I wasn't training, I would help him. The gym at Garfield Park was really small. To get to the gym, you had to walk up a bunch of stairs and go down this small hallway. Once you walked through the double doors, you would see part of a tumbling strip, a junior set of uneven bars, and a junior high bar. The vault runway was in the hallway, which caused you to almost run into the vault when you walked through the double doors. The beam, p-bars (parallel bars), and pommel horse were all tucked into another room off to the side.

While coaching with George, I learned that the gym didn't make the athletes better; coaching did. George's attention to basic gymnastics and presentation built a solid base for just about any gymnast to succeed. These kids needed this program because some of them came from bad situations at home. Some of their parents were addicted to drugs or were not around, or the kids just needed to get away from the violence in their neighborhood. There *may* have been a situation in which one of the gymnasts carried a gun because he needed it to survive walking through the park at night to get home.

It was at this point that I realized George cared about more than just coaching gymnastics; he really cared for the kids. He would do whatever he could to make sure that the kids could afford the already inexpensive gymnastics tuition. This sometimes meant that he would find sponsors for the kids or find creative payment systems for them. He used gymnastics not only to make them better gymnasts, but also to give them better lives. The kids saw what George was doing for them, and in turn, they worked hard for him and got really good at gymnastics. I coached with George for a few years in high school, but disagreements with the park supervisor and the unexpected death of one of the gymnasts from walking pneumonia caused me to quit my job and end my coaching career—at least that's what I thought.

After my shoulder injury in high school, I didn't want anything to do with gymnastics, so I went off to college

(SIU), did a couple years there, and had to come back home. After being at home for a while and driving my mom crazy, she told me I needed to find a *job*. This is where things got a little weird, and now I look back and realize that it was a sign from God.

At the time, I was pretty far removed from gymnastics, but out of the blue, I got a call from the gym owner at Beverly Gymnastics Center. I don't know how she found me, but she called my grandfather's house to see if I wanted to coach gymnastics. At first, it was a hard no, but after remembering what my mom told me, I applied for the job. After getting the job, I remember feeling out of place. I hadn't done any gymnastics or even thought about

gymnastics in years. At this time, I was more into partying, drinking, and other stupid stuff. I had no clue what I was doing, but there was a coach there named Jason

Cardenas, who helped me figure it out. I just needed a little help getting that feel for gymnastics back.

At that time, it was still just a job. I still didn't enjoy the sport. It was just a way to keep my mom off my back and keep a couple of bucks in my pockets. I thought that I was going to make a career out of being a party promoter or being a music executive. Early on at Beverly Gymnastics, I would teach recreational classes just to make sure that I had hours. At one point, I was asked to help with the girls' recreational team program. Not only was I *not* a team coach, but I also had no clue about girls' gymnastics. This was a new challenge for me, and I never backed down from a challenge. I started reading the routine books and watching what the other girls' coach (Hong) was doing with his team. Other than the beam, it turned out the rest of it was just like the gymnastics that I once knew. Floor skills were the same skills that the boys did; vault was pretty much the same too. Uneven bars skills were also very similar, but they just had two bars instead of one. In my head, I would remember things that George would do with me. I remembered that he would always talk about form and presentation, so I made that a big part of what I did. I knew that if I did this, then at least we would look good. He would always focus on our basic skills because once you had a strong knowledge of the basic skills, you could do anything. I trained the girls hard on basic skills, and before I knew it, they were starting to look like pretty good gymnasts. They ended up having a very good season that year!

After my success with the girls, I remember wanting to start a boys' team at Beverly. Although the girls were getting better, I felt that I would be a better boys' coach because I knew more about boys' gymnastics. I went to my boss at Beverly and asked if I could start a boys' team. We didn't have a whole lot of boys in the program at that time, so I found out who was interested and went from there. I was able to find seven boys who wanted to be a part of my journey. Not to disrespect them at all, but they were not my most talented group of gymnasts. Despite not being the most talented, they did enjoy gymnastics and rarely missed practice. While I was getting this team started, I was still coaching girls, but I knew that my future would be in boys' gymnastics.

One day, a group of boys came in to sign up for gymnastics. Little did I know that this was just the beginning of a new crop of boys. Glenn and Chancellor were the first in the group. Then came Jihad, Shareef, Joey, David K., and Malcolm. This group was very talented, and they worked

hard. I loved working with them, and they were really dedicated gymnasts. Not only were they dedicated to the sport, but their parents also became like family to me. We would do dinners together and go on group outings. They were so loyal that when I decided to leave Beverly Gymnastics for a job with the Chicago Park District, they all followed me.

I never intended to work for the Chicago Park District again, but C. J. Johnson gave me a call and told me that his old teammate, Bob Ito, was taking a job as manager of the Chicago Park District gymnastics program. He said that Bob was going to try to do some good things for the program. I believed C. J. because he had always looked out for my best interests, so I applied for the job and accepted the position that I was offered. My boys' team had a new home at Calumet Park on the far Southeast side of Chicago.

The gym wasn't better than what we had at Beverly Gymnastics, but because the tuition was so much cheaper, the boys could train more hours. During this time, I picked up another gymnast, Justin Maxwell, whom I would end up forming a great relationship with. I remember bringing the boys that followed me and the newly inherited boys together for a chat. I wanted to introduce myself and my team to them as well as find out what competitive levels they were. I remember asking Justin, and he shouted out the level that he thought he was going to be. I replied with a very snide comment like, "Not with me you're not." I probably shouldn't have responded like that, but I just had to. As a team, we had some success, but unfortunately, I was injured while spotting one of the boys on still rings. I had surgery to repair my left elbow and was forced to remain out of the gym for six months while I healed. In the meantime, Bob Ito (the reason I returned to the Chicago Park District in the first place) was fired and was replaced by Cindy Morano. After my surgery, I wanted to get back in the gym as soon as possible, but Cindy would not allow it. Even though Cindy and I have a great relationship now, at that time it was like mixing oil and water. We did not see eye to eye, and because of that rocky relationship, she would not help me get back to the gym, even on light duty.

When I was finally allowed back, I was transferred to Harrison Park. I thought I would hate it there because I was going to be working with a tough Romanian coach named Marius. I had seen Marius at competitions, and he always looked so serious. When I finally got there, I was surprised at how nice and funny Marius was. Not only was he a great person, but he was also a great teacher and mentor. I learned

so much from him that I still use today when I'm coaching. My boys' team significantly improved in their new environment. I had some more new boys in the program (Nikko and Trevor) but had lost Glenn and Malcolm to Lakeshore Academy while I was out during my injury.

I stayed at Harrison until both Justin and Chancellor graduated and went to college. After Justin and Chancellor left, the original team kind of broke up. Jihad and Shareef moved to Egypt with their family. Trevor stopped doing gymnastics and focused more on the Jesse White Tumbling Team. I started a new crew at Harrison Park because the show must go on. Around this time, I also started getting

closer to Reggie, another Park District employee. Reggie had been a Park District gymnast but was now a full-time coach. Reggie loved gymnastics, too, and was a very talented young coach. Reggie had some really talented kids on his team, and seeing what he could do with the kids at his gym kept me motivated. Reggie and I went on to be really good friends, and he was even a groomsman in my wedding.

I stayed at the Chicago Park District for a total of twelve years, but toward the end, I started to feel like I was not being appreciated by management. I also had a problem with the pay structure. At the Chicago Park District, everyone made the same amount of money, regardless of whether you were a dedicated team coach who worked on your program even when you were off the clock or you were a recreational coach who  called off just because the sun was too bright that day. I didn't need to be the highest-paid coach, but I did want to be recognized for the accomplishments of the team. Around this time, I was starting to feel like my talent was just being wasted at the Park District. I was losing my drive as a coach and needed a change. Along came Jason Cardenas, my old coworker from Beverly Gymnastics Center.

Jason was leaving his coaching job at the Park District of Oak Park to work for the Chicago Fire Department and wanted me to replace him as a coach because he thought I was a good fit for the program. I wasn't completely sold on taking the job in Oak Park at first, but then Jason told me that the Park District of Oak Park would be building a new, state-of-the-art gymnastics facility. He also told me that the salary structure was different from the union-based salary structure at CPD (Chicago Park District). At Oak Park, pay was based on experience, and if you accomplished your annual goals, you would get a raise! I would be a fool not to take this deal. Pay based on accomplishments and input in the design of a new building? I applied for and accepted the position of program specialist and boys' team head coach at the Park District of Oak Park.

The only gymnast who followed me from CPD to Oak Park this time was Zachary Garcia. Oak Park is where I met Jamie Lapke, the best boss that an employee could ask for. Other than my mother, she was the hardest and most dedicated worker I had ever seen. Jamie looked out for me and made sure that I had everything I needed to create a successful program. This is why I was completely loyal to her, regardless of what others would say. When I got injured (with a torn bicep tendon) while saving a gymnast from falling on her head, Jamie was the first person at the hospital. Not because she had to, but because she cared about her staff that much.

My goal was still to one day own a gymnastics club, but I knew that I didn't have the knowledge or experience to start one on my own yet. I heard from many people in the industry that coaches weren't very good businesspeople, which now I know isn't completely true. I knew I didn't want to fall into this category, so I went about getting as much information as I could so that when the time came, I would be prepared. I began to take a lot of the online courses through USA Gymnastics University geared toward educating coaches about how to run a gymnastics business. When Oak Park sent me to the USA Gymnastics National Congress, I went to as many business lectures as I could attend. I talked to as many gym owners as I could to learn what it took to be successful in the gymnastics business. To get a little more experience, Jillian and I started a mobile gymnastics company called Leaps & Bounds Mobile Gymnastics and Tumbling. We bought some mats and bars, and with the help of my cousin Bert, we bought a van that we used to transport the equipment from school to school. We were able to get firsthand experience on how a gymnastics business was run, and now we just had to wait for our time to come.

After six years of working at Oak Park, I eventually had the opportunity to buy a gym of my own. I refused to leave Jamie in a bad position, so I stayed on with Oak Park until they were able to find a replacement for me. This meant that for six months, I had to run my new gym, work full time at Oak Park, and run my mobile gymnastics business. I really enjoyed my time at Oak Park and the boys I worked with there (Owen, Patrick, Zach, Thanos, Bodhi, Conner, Nick, Linus, and Austin). I also became close with some of my coworkers, and while we didn't always see eye to eye, most of the times were really fun and memorable.

When I bought Prairie Gymnastics Club, there was an existing boys' program with a talented boys' coaching staff. There was no need for me to coach boys, so I went back to my roots and began coaching the girls' team. It had been a while since I had coached girls, but I was able to get back into the swing of things quickly. It was much different from coaching boys, because girls were a lot more focused than boys. When coaching boys, especially young boys, it's more like herding cats. But when coaching girls, you notice that they actually pay attention to you when you are talking; when you turn your back, they are still working. I really enjoyed the change, but I didn't like going to the girls' meets as much because the girls' coaches were way too intense. I still coach at my gym too. Now I coach the girls' team and boys' team, and my favorite classes to teach are preschool classes. I have a new goal with coaching now, which is to create good human beings.

PARALLEL BARS:

Turning My Life Around

PREVIOUSLY TOUCHED ON HOW JILLIAN AND I met, but it's now time to get into how it all went down and turned into what it is today. So I first heard Jillian's voice while talking to her friend Kateura, who I met while visiting my friend George (G.) at his junior college in Champaign. Kateura turned out to be a really good friend of mine. I had been talking to her about how I was trying to slow my lifestyle down a little bit. The partying and other activities were starting to take a toll on me. I was realizing that I needed to be on a different path than the one I was currently on because it wouldn't lead to a positive outcome. So one day while talking on the phone with Kateura, I heard this voice in the background that I had never heard before while talking to her. I said, "Hey, who is that over there?" And immediately Kateura was like, "That's Jill, and no, you can't talk to her because she's too nice for you!"

I probably should have been offended by that comment, but I wasn't. She was probably right. I wasn't the best person to be involved with from the female point of view.

You see, at this time, I didn't really believe in love. I hadn't really seen many relationships that lasted that long. I had definitely seen more divorces than successful marriages. The first example was my parents, who got divorced when I was young. Although their divorce wasn't as bad as some that you see on television, the arguing and stuff that took place had a lasting effect on me. In my young mind, it was the worst thing ever. I went from being able to see my dad (who I always refer to as Butch) every day to seeing him every once in a while. Before I get too far into this story, I would like to say that Butch and Ann tried to keep many things the same for me. There was never a change for me in gymnastics. They made sure that gymnastics was always paid for, which is probably why gymnastics was my safe space for a long time. OK, let me get back to my thoughts on what kind of effect their divorce had on me: enough of an effect that my goal was to never get married. I didn't want to get married, and I didn't want kids because I didn't want to "ruin" anyone's life if there was ever a divorce.

I also had some thoughts about love. In my house, we didn't really say "I love you" a lot. That doesn't mean that we didn't love each other; we just didn't say it a lot. I think the only person I consistently heard say "I love you" in my family was my Aunt Neicy. She would end every—and I mean, *every*—conversation with "Love you, man!" She still does that to this day. I actually had a problem saying "I love you" to anyone for a long time (even to my Aunt Neicy). The words just never felt right coming out of my mouth. The first problem that I had with it was that people threw "I love you" out way too freely. I felt that "I love you" should be special, should be said when you truly meant it and not just because you were ending a phone call. But that's not what I would see. I would hear some of my guys telling five different girls that they loved them but wouldn't mean it to one of them. I would see so many people get married and say before God and all the other witnesses that they loved their soon-to-be spouse but would later go through a divorce and treat that person whom they "loved" worse than a stranger on the street.

My goal was to only say "I love you" to the woman I planned to marry. My problem was that I loved girls, but I hated relationships. I didn't want to have to lie to people about how I truly felt about relationships I was in because no one would ever want to be with me, and that wasn't realistic.

So I did have lots of relationships, but usually when it got too serious, I would do something to sabotage it. I didn't like to hurt people's feelings, so I felt like if I did something stupid, then eventually they would break up with me. I know that this was really terrible, and I'm sorry to anyone that I hurt or led on by doing this.

This explains what Kateura was talking about when she mentioned that Jill (who I always call Jillian) was too nice for me. She knew my track record and was trying to look out for her friend. What she didn't know was that I really was just looking for someone else to talk to who was different from the people I was currently dealing with. I was sick of people asking about what kind of rims were on my car or how much money I had. You see, I had never seen Jillian, but when I heard her voice, I knew she was a white girl. At the time, I wasn't looking for a relationship or anything. I just wanted someone else to talk to, and someone who didn't know anything about me. I wanted someone who would let me be myself.. I didn't have to be tough; I didn't have to be the life of the party. I could actually be me. I'm not trying to say that another Black girl couldn't have these same conversations that I had with Jillian, but something just was telling me that I needed to talk to her. And that day, Kateura kept her word and did not let me talk to her.

Then one day when I was talking to Kateura, Jillian was around again, but this time, Kateura allowed me to speak to her, and we ended up exchanging phone numbers. The conversations were different, like I expected. Jillian seemed to actually care what I was talking about. At that time, she was in college, studying to become a social worker. From that point on, we would talk every day, to the point where my friends Teefa and A. J. would call me "Dunkin'" because they said that I would always be caking (talking about sweet things) with Jillian all the time. When I say we talked all the time, I mean that we would either be texting or talking all day long.

Jillian and I spoke on the phone for about six months before actually meeting each other. When we finally did meet, I immediately knew she was the one for me. The only problem was that I had never really brought anyone around I was dating who was white. What would people think about her? Would my family accept her? More importantly, what would my mother have to say about this? To my surprise, my family was super supportive. They loved Jillian, so my mind was at ease. Her family was great too. Were there people on both sides that our relationship had to grow on? Yes, but no one was ever rude about it. In the beginning, there were times that I was an idiot, but she stuck with me through those times. No one besides my mother had stuck by my side like Jillian did.

I remember when I finally decided that I should ask her to marry me. We had been together about eight years. She had never given me a hard time about me not asking, but she had definitely started to throw around some hints from time to time. One day I just woke up and decided that today would be the day. I called up my guy Ahmand and was like, "Go to the jewelry store with me."

He said, "For what?"

Maybe he thought that I was going to buy myself some new jewelry or something. When I told him that I was going to buy a ring for Jillian, he laughed at me harder than I had ever heard him laugh. I couldn't blame him because I had always told him that I was never getting married. After he finished laughing and realized that I was serious, he agreed to come with me. I also called my guy Scotty, because he also needed to be with me for this special occasion. This didn't go without any drama though. When we got to the jewelry store and picked out the perfect ring, the jeweler ran my debit card for the purchase, and the card was declined. Talk about an embarrassing moment. Why did this happen? I knew I had the funds available. Why was this happening to me? Then I got a text message from my bank about a fraud alert. A large purchase was being made, and they wanted to make sure it was me. Crisis averted; it was just my bank protecting my funds. I can laugh about that now, but at the time I was sick to my stomach.

So now I had a ring, but how was I going to ask her to be my wife? I am not the most romantic guy at all, but I had to make this special for her. I had to step outside my comfort zone for a second. So I came up with the perfect plan for when I would pop the question. I did the traditional thing by asking her dad for his blessing, and he was excited. Her birthday was coming up, so I decided I would do it at her birthday party. The day of the party came, and her sisters, parents, and other family members were there. She should have known something was up because some of my family and friends were there too. I told her that I had to get her gift out of the car and that she should come with me to get it. That makes no sense to me now, but that's what I said. When we got to the car, I asked her to get the gift out of the car.

She looked in the car, and when she turned around because she didn't see a gift, I was down on one knee. I asked her if she would marry me, and her first response before she said yes was "About time." I couldn't do anything but laugh because she was right. I did take way too long to get to this point, but I did finally get there.

We went back inside the bar, where she was happy to show off her new ring. Our plan (meaning Jillian's plan) was to be engaged for eighteen months. She planned the wedding better than any wedding planner ever could. I never knew how much a wedding could cost, but I definitely found out. I think we went like fifteen thousand dollars over our original budget, but it was worth every penny. Just about everyone who was important to us was there. I may be biased, but it is the best wedding that I have ever been to. And not to toot my own horn too much, but my groom's speech was on its way to being the best ever—until I was rudely cut off by my new wife. Ha! Apparently, the food was ready to be served, and it was getting cold.

After things had settled down and we went on about life, we decided that it was time to expand our family. We tried for a while, and nothing was happening, so we found a fertility doctor to see what was going on. This was one of the best fertility doctors in the area, so we gave him a shot. We did all the treatments and IVF stuff (in vitro fertilization), and none of it worked. The doctors eventually told us that Jillian had "bad eggs" and wouldn't be able to conceive a child. First of all, it was hard enough for me to see her going through everything she had to go through with all of the IVF stuff. I mean, every time it didn't work, the look on her face hurt me. And now hearing this from the doctor just killed me. We both struggled with this, but she was taking it very hard. I don't know if she realized how hard I was taking it, but I hated that there was nothing I could do to help her. I have always prided myself on being able to fix things, but I had no solution for this. Maybe God was trying to let me know that he was in control of this.

We had one more possible solution for this situation. There was an option to get an egg donor. With this process, you pick the person who will donate "good eggs" to you. You see how they look, what color eyes, family history, and all that. By the way, this is also not cheap and not covered by insurance. You have to pay for the donor's checkups,  travel—and, yes, also their eggs. This process was going to cost us well over $20,000. Right before we were about to pay for an egg donor, God gave us Olivia. Let me tell you how Jillian told me about this great news. I came home from work, and I walked up the stairs in our apartment. On the top of the stairs was this teddy bear with a pregnancy test on it. Now here's a view into a guy's brain. The first thing I thought was that one of her sisters was pregnant. So I'm like, "What's that for?" Then she told me that she was pregnant and had gone to the doctor and got a pregnancy test to verify it. This was one of the happiest days of my life. I remember telling our families, and they were so happy. I don't know if I ever mentioned this to anyone, but another reason that I was sad about us not being able to conceive a child was because if I didn't have a child, not only would Jillian not be a mother, but my mom would also never experience being a grandmother. To me, I would have let down two of the most important people in my life.

We finally had Olivia, our only child, and she is beautiful. A little busy from time to time, but great nonetheless. Having Olivia changed a lot of things for me. Once I saw her being born, I knew my life would never be the same. I have experienced love before. I love my parents;

I love my wife, Jillian; but the love that I have for Olivia can't be described. When I look at her now that she is growing up, I can see a lot of myself in the way she acts. She's silly, just like me. She is super sassy, just like me, and she is also very creative, just like me. Over the summer, she wanted to get a skateboard, and because we weren't getting it for her, she decided to get the money for it herself. She went into the office at the gym, found an empty box, and decorated it. When she brought the box out, she had turned it into a storefront. She had gotten this bracelet-making kit as a gift and decided that she would sell bracelets that she made at her new store. This was a proud-dad moment for me and reminded me of what I had done as a kid when I started selling tie-dyed T-shirts.

The reason that I work so hard now is so Olivia can have all the things that I didn't have growing up. I want to make sure that Olivia never has to grow up in an environment like I grew up in. I do worry sometimes about how she will get treated because she is mixed. I wonder how much I should teach her about her Black roots. Will the things that she learns about slavery make her feel anger toward the white side of her family? How will she get treated by her Black friends because she's half white, and how will she get treated by her white friends because she's half Black? When am I going to have to have the conversation about the N-word? These are all things that I struggle with, but when the time comes, I'm sure that I will find the perfect words to help her get through these times. One thing that I do know is that I will do whatever needs to be done to protect my best friends, Jillian and Olivia.

The next thing Jillian did really let me know that she was the one for me. You see, I had an opportunity to fulfill my lifelong goal of owning a gymnastics gym. I was having a drink with another coach after a gymnastics competition with my Oak Park team. During our conversation, he asked me if I ever had thought about owning a gymnastics club. Of course I had! Jillian and I had written a business plan for a gym that we wanted to start one day. This would be a better situation than starting from scratch because this particular gym was already established and also came with a pretty large men's gymnastics competition. I called Jillian and was like, "You want to buy a gymnastics gym?" and without any hesitation at all, she said yes. We started the process and became gym owners in about six months. The tricky part was that we took over Prairie Gymnastics in January of 2018, but I was in the middle of my competition season, and as I previously mentioned, I didn't want to leave my manager, Jamie, without a coach. I still had my boys' team at the Park District of Oak Park and had boys who would qualify for Junior National Championships. So to make this happen, Jillian left her job of twelve years, and without any business experience, she took over as the owner of Prairie alone until I finished my season at Oak Park. I was also blessed to have Jamie, a very understanding boss, who would allow me to take care of things at Prairie if I needed to be there to handle something business related.

I enjoy married life. It isn't always perfect, but I kind of knew that going into it. Jillian and I are from very different backgrounds, and of course, that would cause us to bump heads from time to time. I think all new families go through that, but I think I was going through something different. When we argued sometimes, I would get way too upset. Some of the smallest things would trigger me, and I would act a damn fool. I hated being like that. It was not the person I was. I would never get physical or anything, but I hated how she looked when I got angry. She would look at me with so much fear in her eyes. I definitely knew if we wanted to have a happy family, I didn't want to be that person. The anger I felt reminded me of how I felt in high school when the lady blew her horn at me and I blew up. I had gone to anger management classes before, but honestly, I never took it seriously. You see, back then, that anger and aggressiveness kept me safe in the streets. The times in college when I would just blow up and fight were applauded by my peers. I knew I could handle myself if things ever went sideways. But now I didn't have to be this way. There was no one I needed to protect myself from, so why was this still happening?

I decided to see a therapist again, but this time I wanted my therapist to be someone who looked like me. This person had to be able to relate to the things that I saw and did growing up. I talked to Jillian about the way I was feeling, and she used her social worker connections (she had her master's degree in social work by this time) to help find the right person for me. The therapist I chose was named Matt, and he just happened to grow up on the Southeast side of Chicago in Terror Town, a pretty rough part of Chicago. When I went to see him, he let me be as open as possible and didn't seem to be judging me or looking at me like I was a monster. I talked to him about all the deaths that I had dealt with in my life: my best friend from first grade was killed; my friend in high school committed suicide; my other friend Baby D. was murdered during winter break my freshman year in college; not too long after that, my friend Snoop was murdered; my grandfather, whom I was really close to, died; and my Uncle Robert was murdered when I was a young kid too. When my Uncle Robert was killed, this affected me so much that at the time it happened, my kindergarten teacher thought I was slow because when she asked me to draw a man, I drew a box. They brought my parents up to the school and everything, and when they asked me why I drew the box instead of a man, I told them because the man was inside the box like my uncle. There was also my good friend Akil. Akil was murdered shortly after our freshman year in college too. He was shot and killed after someone broke into his house. Also, my Uncle Terry (my dad's younger brother) was stabbed to death by his girlfriend. When my dad and I went to his apartment to clean out his things, we could still see the spot where he took his final breath. Then there was my friend Tracey, a.k.a. Pinkhouse, who died after suffering two massive strokes. Tracey had been my barber but also became a great friend.

Matt (my therapist) talked to me about how I was also suppressing my feelings about my parents getting divorced. I had never really told anyone about how I felt about any of this. I just held on to it. I had gotten to the point where I didn't really feel anything anymore. For a long time, I didn't really care about death. It was like whatever was going to happen just happened. I remember going to my grandmother's funeral and not feeling anything. I wasn't sad, I wasn't crying, I was just there. This actually made me really nervous because that wasn't normal. When I met Jillian and we got married, I was trying to have feelings again, and all these previously suppressed emotions just started coming out.

My therapist can also be credited with my writing this book. He felt that putting all this out there would be therapeutic for me, and he was right. I feel that other Black males should also find a way to deal with mental health issues. I was recently on a panel at an event that my publishing company (SHE Publishing LLC) put together on the topic of Black men and mental health. I was shocked to see how many of us on the panel had the same story. This is a huge problem in our community, and some light needs to be shed on this. You see, when we grow up, we are taught that we have to be tough. As a little kid, if you fall down and hurt yourself, you better get up, dust yourself off, and keep it moving. We're taught that we can't show emotions because that is a sign of weakness. And for those who don't know, showing emotions in an environment like I grew up in can get you hurt. I was asked a thought-provoking question while on this mental health panel: "What would you tell a young Darion about how to deal with mental health?" My answer was, "I don't know if I would tell him anything different because he still had to survive in the same environment." I think now in 2023, as I'm writing this book, people are becoming more aware of mental health issues. I just hope how my people feel about dealing with it also changes with the times.

There is another thing that I would like to discuss that needs some attention. It's the question that some people want to know but may be scared to ask. How is it being in an interracial relationship (marriage)? This has definitely been a topic of conversation with my therapist on several occasions. The transition into a different type of family environment has not been the easiest for me. Sometimes I feel like people are always judging us. I feel like I'm not black enough for the Black people, and of course I'm not white enough for the white people. This may only be in my head, but it feels like I can't just be who I am. When I'm around some of my guys, they expect me to be how I was when I was younger and acting a fool in the clubs. On the other hand, I feel like I have to watch the things I talk about around white people because I will be judged by the things I say. I tend to watch the way I say things in these situations because people who didn't grow up like I did may not understand the slang terms that I grew up using. Or when I come around my people, now they say I talk like a white boy. I have learned how to be somewhat of a chameleon, being able to adapt to any situation. Now my family and I live in the western suburbs of Chicago. Although it's only about forty minutes outside the city, it's like traveling to another state for people who don't really leave the neighborhood that often.

It's also hard for me because Ann (my mom) and Bubba (my stepfather) live in Mississippi, my dad (Butch) lives in the city, and most of my friends still stay on the Southside of Chicago. This means that I don't get to see people I'm close to who look like me very often. Don't get me wrong; I don't mind being around Jillian's family. There are some that I truly enjoy being around, especially Frank (Jillian's stepfather), but it's hard being so far away from my people. I sit around a lot of the time and just miss my friends. For a long time, I didn't go into the city and hang out with my people because Jillian was scared for me to be in the city. She knew the areas I went to weren't safe, but what she didn't remember was that I have navigated these dangerous neighborhoods all my life. I was really struggling with this new life and had to find some balance. I feel that I was angry a lot because I was around Jillian's family all the time and didn't spend any time with my family and friends. It really started getting hard around the holidays. I'm not a big holiday person, but after spending so many holidays with Jillian's family, I started missing the family dinners that we used to have. I missed having greens, dressing, and macaroni and cheese. I needed some soul food in my life—no more casseroles for me. I talked to Jillian about the way I was feeling, and she came up with the idea of going to visit my mom in Mississippi for Thanksgiving. We have done that for the last few years now, and I can feel my energy changing. When in an interracial relationship (or any relationship), you must make sure to try to respect each other's culture as well as balance the time with each other's families.

HORIZONTAL BAR:

From Employee to Employer

HOW DID I BECOME A "BUSINESSMAN"? THERE are a few things that let me know I didn't want to work for someone else. First, for those who really know me, they know that I don't do well with authority, ha. I don't really enjoy people telling me what I can and cannot do. If someone tells me that I can't do something, I immediately want to know, "Why not?" Next, when I saw people go to work on TV, they had to wear some kind of suit or uniform. At this time, I did *not* like to dress up (suit jackets, ties, or dress shoes). These items of clothing were so uncomfortable to me, and when I wore a tie (which was probably a clip-on tie), it would pinch my neck. I hated wearing clothes that looked like everyone else's, so uniforms weren't going to work either. When I went shopping for clothes as a young teen, I remember looking for things that no one else had, even if this was not the coolest thing to do. If I wasn't the only person wearing something, I at least wanted to be the first person to wear it. In my mind, the only way to control my work attire would be to own the place where I would work.

There was another thing that made me realize I needed to own my own business. I loved to make my own money! I didn't like someone else to tell me how much I would get paid. I wanted to be in control of how much money I could make and not be limited to a salary. Some people like the security of having a paycheck, but that's just not for me. If someone is paying you a salary, then they are also telling you when and where you have to work. I have always been an entrepreneur as far back as I can remember. As a kid, I would always want to find new ways to make my own money. I remember watching this educational show for kids and seeing them teach people how to tie-dye shirts. I thought that this was so cool, and if I could figure out how to do this, I could sell the shirts and make some money. I asked my mom for some money. I went to Walgreens and bought some dye and rubber bands. So now I had everything I needed except for the shirts to dye. So what did I do? I took some of my uncle's shirts (at this time we lived with my grandfather and a couple of my uncles), dyed the shirts, and sold them to family members who could fit in the shirts. Let's just say that my uncle wasn't happy about his shirts that were missing, but he did buy a couple of cool new tie-dyed shirts that just happened to fit him perfectly. These first initial sales gave me enough money to purchase other shirts to sell, and I was able to make a few bucks.

I was also fascinated by the dope boys in the neighborhood. Although I knew what they were doing was wrong, there was something about their drive that caught my attention. To be honest, they were the only "successful" people who I actually knew. I had seen superstars on TV buying cars, jewelry, and fancy cars, but they weren't real. The guys on the block were people I could see every day, and I could see how, on the top layer, they looked happy.

In high school my entrepreneurial spirit was alive and wanting to figure out something to do. In the early '90s, pagers (we called them beepers) were the coolest thing to own as an urban teenager. They weren't popular because all the brain surgeons had them. They were popular because back then, all the dope boys had them in the hood, and so did all the rappers. And who started most of the fashion trends of this time? You guessed it: the rappers and dope boys. Another thing to know about me is that I like cool electronics, and again, I like to be the first one to have things.

I saved some money, and I found a guy named John B. whom I could get a pager from. I would go to his shop and pay my bill every month. I would go in the shop and look at the other cool pagers that I couldn't afford. One day John B. came up to me and asked if I thought any of my friends would want a pager. I knew that my friends would want them, but my first question to John B. was, "Can I make any money from this?" He was willing to let me make a "referral fee" from everyone I referred to him. This arrangement went well for a while, but then I wanted to figure out a way to make more money. I realized that when everyone bought a pager, they also had to pay the monthly airtime fee. John B. was getting all the new pager sales *and* all the airtime fees. I figured that since this new revenue was coming from my connections, I should be receiving something from this. John B. was a very reasonable man, and he did give me a few more bucks for these referrals. This probably went on all throughout my high school years and only really stopped because John B. sold his shop and moved to Florida.

In college I dibbled and dabbled in a few things but came to realize that I loved putting on events. As I mentioned earlier, I joined a fraternity while attending SIU. One of my brothers (Kevin) was already into putting together events. One of our first events that we put on together as an organization was a concert with the famous hip-hop duo Outkast. I was able to see how an event was organized from beginning to end. This event would lay the groundwork for things that I would do later in my business journey.

After my short two-year stint at SIU, I went back home to Chicago. While back in Chicago, I connected with some fraternity brothers who were attending Chicago State University. I spent *a lot* of time with these brothers, especially my brother Charles (now known as Karim). Karim was an entrepreneur like myself who also liked putting on events. He was a true hustler. We did all kinds of things (legally) to make money for the organization and then for ourselves. We did comedy shows, hair shows, and all kinds of other events. We did these for a while before branching off and doing other things, but one thing that I can say that I learned from Karim was to never give up.

I put together another team after working with the brothers. This team consisted of my old gymnastics teammate Scotty and my friend Ahmand from the Circle. We all had that hustler mentality, and I felt that we would work well together. Boy, was I right! We started working on an event right away. We were going to do a comedy show at this club called Honeysuckle. It was a nice location, but they didn't have a license to sell liquor. I hooked up with a friend I had made while attending SIU who was now a comedian named Da Wildcat. Wildcat would be the host of the show and was in charge of finding other comedians to do the shows, while the rest of us would iron out the other details. Ahmand found a way to get around the whole liquor license problem. He had learned from someone else that the liquor license just gave the establishment the right to sell liquor, but if people brought their own liquor, we were still "legal." What Ahmand suggested was a technique that I think he learned from his father-in-law, which was to sell "setups." You see, we didn't allow any outside chasers (things to mix with hard liquor) or cups. So we sold four cups and a bowl of ice for $5 each. The funny thing is, we probably made more money off setups than we made off ticket sales—ha! The show would have been a success if it wasn't for a fight that ended the show a little early. We did a few other events after that show, but after a while, this team split up. My business dreams were not over, and this was just a stepping stone for what was to come.

I learned that when one thing doesn't go as expected, I had to pivot to a different plan because things don't stop. I think my drive and fearless attitude were instilled in me from things that I learned on the streets. What I learned from all the life-threatening situations that I had been involved in is that what doesn't kill you only makes you stronger. When I was negotiating the deal to buy the gym that meant me realizing my dream, I was able to stay nice and calm because I knew that if it didn't work, the skills that I had as a gymnastics coach would allow me to find another coaching job. When we were going through the pandemic and had no revenue coming in, I didn't panic because I'd been poor before and saw my parents provide for me with less. I've been around murderers and robbers damn near all my life, so if you are not one of those people, I don't feel there is anything you can do to me to stop me.

I take this fearless attitude into every situation, and it has been good to me so far. A prime example is when I planned to add a girls' competition to my historically all-boys gymnastics competition that was previously held at the Credit Union 1 Arena (formerly the UIC Pavilion). I received a phone call one day from the director of operations of the facility. He informed me that not only did I not have a guaranteed contract for the venue, but there was also no guarantee that I could rent the facility in the future either. So, to say the least, this really sucked. I had already begun promoting a boys' competition as well as a girls' competition that would take place on the same weekend at another venue on the UIC campus. I was stumped for a second but realized just a year before I had received an email from the sales director at Navy Pier. I reached out immediately (within an hour of receiving the news from UIC) and was notified that there may be an opening for the weekend that I wanted, but they would have to check the calendar and get back to me. The very next day I received a call letting me know the space was available! There were two options for us, Festival Hall A (which is 113,000 square feet and would be approximately $60,000) or Festival Hall B (which was 60,000 square feet and about $35,000). I decided that we would choose Festival

Hall B, but when my team made a layout of the equipment, we realized that the equipment that we needed wouldn't fit. Without panicking I reached out to Navy Pier, and we were able to work out a deal that worked for both parties. The only problem was, I still didn't know how I would pay for the space. We had never done a girls' competition, so I had no clue if anyone would even show up. I had to reach back to my party-promoting days and do some old-fashioned guerilla marketing. We created logos that would catch the eye of the girls' coaches, and our graphic designer created flyers that made it look like this was a competition that you had to attend. I also played on the fact that there was once a huge girls' competition at Navy Pier that was no longer taking place and knew that people were dying to get back into that iconic venue. We planned on getting about four hundred girls that first year and hoped for more in the future. The day that registration started, my meet director and I opened up our computers and crossed our fingers in the hope that we would get a couple of registrations on that first day. To our surprise, we got over eight hundred registrations within the first few hours. It happened so quickly, I got nervous that we wouldn't be able to handle it, and I shut down registration. I ended up renting some more equipment so that we could add a few more girls. I opened up registration again and added four hundred more girls for a total of twelve hundred girls. This was a far greater turnout than the original four hundred that we were expecting. For the first year in our new home, we had almost twenty-three hundred athletes as well as six men's college teams.

The beginning of gym ownership wasn't without its issues. You see, the previous gym owners stayed on as coaches to help with the transition. Some people told me that this was not a good idea, but of course we didn't listen. I think the former owners meant well, but Jillian and I had a different vision than they did. They, too, loved gymnastics, but they were older and didn't have any children. We had

Olivia, so we had to have more of a focus on making money to plan for her future as well as our own. We wanted to focus on a recreational program and create a family-friendly environment, while they seemed to be more focused on creating high-level teams. This wasn't a bad thing, but our goals just didn't align, and we had to part ways in our business relationship.

Jillian is the reason why our gym is so successful now. Even though, going into gym ownership, she didn't have a lot of gymnastics experience, what she did have was her organizational skills and her motherly instincts. She knows what mothers want and how hard their day is, and she based what we did on what they needed. For example, the previous owners had offered in-person registration only. Jillian thought about a mom having to lug her kids to the gym and get them in and out of car seats, so she made sure that registration could be done online at their convenience. She made Prairie a place where families could be comfortable and a place that caters to their needs within reason. Some of this has rubbed off on me, but I'm still a work in progress. One day I hope I can be half as good as she is.

Shortly after we purchased the gym, we began having more success. Although our team enrollment declined initially, our recreational and preschool enrollment almost tripled. Our gym seemed to be getting a positive reputation in the community. We were becoming a more family-friendly gym, and I have to give that credit to Jillian. Although she doesn't give herself credit for being a businesswoman, it was her instincts that made the gym grow into what we have today. At first, I was nervous about working with my wife, but I think what we do works for us. She takes care of all things that make the gym work in the front of the house, and I handle what happens on the floor. I just try to make sure that she doesn't have to teach any classes, because I know she hates doing that.

Now that the gym is doing well and the Windy City Invitational is showing constant growth, I have time to focus on other business ideas that will help generate more revenue so that I can one day give Olivia experiences that I did not have when I was younger, and make sure that she does not have to grow up in places similar to where I grew up. None of this was easy, and there were a lot of long days to get to this point. I've heard that if you love what you do, you'll never work a day in your life. That saying is BS, because I love what I do, but I have had a bunch of hard days at work. There are the days when you feel you can't do one more thing, but then you have to do one more thing. You have the days when you are sick as a dog, but you still have to go in because if you don't work, then a lot of people who depend on you don't eat. That can be the scariest part about being a "boss." So many people depend on you so their families can survive. That is a whole lot of pressure. You have to be crazy to want to put that much pressure on yourself, but I think I may be a little crazy. That pressure is what drives me. The pressure of not letting my staff down drives me. The pressure of not letting my parents down drives me. The pressure of making sure Jillian and Olivia can live the way that they want to drives me to want to be great and to keep pushing forward.

AWARDS:
It Took a Village

I WANT TO START THIS FINAL CHAPTER BY SAYING that I have always had two fears (Olivia, I know I say to not be scared of anything, but bear with me): a fear of heights and a fear of failure. Heights, although they still make me a little nervous, I can get past. But the fear of failure has always been a struggle for me. The reason is because if I fail, I let people down. The look on a person's face when they are disappointed just kills me. The reason that I worked so hard at gymnastics was because I didn't want to disappoint anyone who helped me get to where I was in gymnastics. It wasn't just in gymnastics though; it was in everything I did. After gymnastics, I think I became a person who let a lot of people down. I wasn't living up to what people expected of me, or what I expected of myself. That is because I was missing a very big part of who I was.

God gave me gymnastics as my gift. There were a lot of reasons that I shouldn't have been good at gymnastics. Reason number one: I was a Black male from the inner city, where there were very few gymnastics centers. Reason number two: we were poor, and the money that my parents made should have gone to other things that we needed. Reason number three: I was bigger than the average male gymnast. When I was training for the Olympics my sophomore year in high school, I was five feet ten and weighed about 175 pounds. I was built more like a football player than any gymnast I knew of at that time. Despite all that, I was really good at gymnastics. This is probably the first time I have ever said that. My normal response when people say, "I heard that you were really good at gymnastics" is "I was OK." I was good at gymnastics because I was supposed to be. Gymnastics was and is my passion and purpose.

My success allowed me to be in some of the gymnastics circles that I am in today. I'm a member of the USA Gymnastics Events staff, which allows me to help organize some of the top gymnastics competitions in the world. I'm a member of the Illinois Boys Elite coaching staff and the treasurer of the Illinois Men's Gymnastics program. I'm also a member of the National Gymnastics Judges Association. Another thing that my success allowed me to be is a coach. Coaching gave me the platform to positively impact the lives of children. You see, I don't coach to win awards; I use this sport to prepare my students for the things life has to offer. When I coach, my practices are all assignment-based. I give them an assignment, and it is up to them to complete it. Now I guide them along the way, and if they complete their assignments, they will enjoy the success that comes with it. If they don't complete them, then they have to take ownership of the consequences of not completing that task. The consequence could be not doing well in competition or letting their parents know why they aren't showing the progress that they should be showing. Either way, they learn to own up to their responsibilities. That is why I love this sport—although I didn't realize how much gymnastics truly meant to me until I didn't have it; I was lost until I found it again. Once I found it again, my life started to turn around because the missing part that would reconnect me to my true path was whole again.

As I write this, I'm actually on a flight back from San Jose, California, after being on the USA Gymnastics Event staff for US Championships. At the same time, I'm planning for my gymnastics competition, which is being held at Navy Pier in Chicago. It is one of the largest gymnastics competitions in the country, hosting over twenty-five hundred gymnasts annually. This, coming from a Black man who came from one of the most violent neighborhoods in the country, is quite the accomplishment.

I've frequently heard the saying, "It takes a village to raise a child." I totally agree with the statement and know for a fact that I wouldn't be here if it wasn't for God and my "village." My village began with a strong mother who started from nothing and went on to earn a PhD in early childhood development. A woman who had to raise her brothers and sisters because her mom died when she was young. A woman who had to raise me in the inner city of Chicago with gang violence and other influences all around. A woman who had to deal with me through my teenage years and early twenties, when I thought that I knew everything about everything.

My "village" also included my father, who taught me what a father was. He also grew up in a rough and tough environment. Since his dad was not around, he had to take care of his brothers

and sisters. My Aunt Nikita says that she never really missed not having her dad around, "because Butch was there to fill in." Growing up, not only did he make sure I had what I needed, but he also tried as hard as he could to give me the things that I wanted. When my parents got divorced, he paid child support long after he had to. He was also my first business mentor. I watched him buy and sell property around the Chicago area. He did this without any formal business training. I was exposed to various types of music and other forms of the arts because he didn't want me to be limited to the things that I saw around me. Although my father and I aren't really emotional guys, I know how much he cares about me, and I hope he knows how much I love him.

My "village" also included my grandfather Albert Moore (Daddy Mo'). He was a great man whom I miss so much. Although he had his issues, he still gave me the best advice. He taught me the importance of being there for your family. He is also one of the reasons that I am so observant. He knew everything that was going on around him at all times, and I use that skill too. The only real problem that my grandfather and I had was that he cheered for the wrong Chicago baseball team (the Cubs). But all kidding aside, I wish he was here to see me now. I know that he is looking down on me right now and smiling.

My village also includes my wife, Jillian, and daughter, Olivia. Jillian sacrificed everything so that I could realize my

dream, and Olivia sacrifices time with me so that I can continue to live out my dreams. I hope that they know that all my hard work isn't for me. I want to make sure that they have everything that I didn't have when I was growing up. I don't want them to have to see the things that I saw growing up in Chicago. There are a lot of things that I have done that

I am not proud of, but hopefully the man that I am today makes up for that.

There are also my family members who stepped in to make sure that I wasn't able to stray too far off the right path.

 My Uncle Clay and Aunt Lue don't know how much it means for me to answer the phone on my birthday each year to hear them singing, "Happy Birthday," which they still do to this day. Aunt Lue being in the hospital with my mom and being her support system when I was born means a lot to me. My Uncle Clay retired from the Chicago Fire Department and is now experiencing some health issues, but he still calls me from time to time to check up on me. My Uncle Tonio (who has passed on now) took time out of his day (along with his friend Vick) to make sure I got to gymnastics practice. There were

my Uncle Fred and Uncle Lamont, whom I looked up to on the athletic side because they were good at every sport. My Uncle Steve had a work ethic like no other. He is one of the reasons that I work so hard. My Aunt Bett (Sharon) was an example of success. She was the first person in our family to live in a high-rise that wasn't the projects. I remember being so happy every time we went to visit her downtown condo. There was also my "cousin" Dennis, who showed me what a true hustler was. He made things happen by any means necessary. He isn't my family by blood, but he has always treated me as if I were a blood relative. We don't talk as much as we used to because we are both so busy, but I want him to know how much our friendship means to me. There was also my cousin Bert, who believed in me when I wanted to start my gymnastics business. He helped buy a van for Jillian and me when we wanted to start our mobile gymnastics program. He also made me so proud when he got his degree in engineering from the University of Memphis after growing up in a house with an outhouse in Mariana, Arkansas. He is one of the smartest people I know; his dedication to success is unmatched by anyone I know.

There are many others in my village, including two former gymnasts of mine. The first is Chancellor Foulks, whose dad (Kevin) I talked about in the introduction. Chancellor is someone who I look up to. You see, Chancellor reminds me so much of his dad. Chancellor is a very intelligent young man. From what I can see, he is a great husband, dad, son, and businessman. He owns a few chiropractic clinics in Texas and will soon be opening more. Another former athlete is Justin Maxwell, who quit his logistics job to join his wife in starting a marketing and branding company. He is also a great husband, dad, and son. If I had a son, these are two individuals I would love for my sons to be like.

My village also includes Scotty, my former teammate, the best man at my wedding, and Olivia's godfather. We have been friends for a very long time. He's someone who has also had to overcome a lot of things and is now successful in the real estate industry. I admire how he is able to pivot when something may not go well and turn that into something more

 successful. Finally, there are Ahmand and his wife, Robiar, who had a family early and struggled to make ends meet, but now they have a very successful pest control company (RB Pest Solutions). Robiar is the first Black woman to have a pest control product called Bug Strike (shameless plug) in Home Depot. Ahmand's parents used to find comfort that I was a mentor to Ahmand and kept him safe, but now the roles have reversed, and I look up to him for the things that he's accomplished.

I would be remiss if I didn't include one more person: my great-grandfather Fred Daniels. He was a Black man who

owned over two hundred acres of land in Arkansas when Black people weren't supposed to be able to do this. My mom told me that he sold butter and beef to be able to purchase this land. I remember taking trips to Arkansas to visit him during the summer. Once you made it to his house, you could look in any direction, and as far as you could see, he owned everything. I didn't realize at that time how great that was, but now as a grown man, I am truly impressed by what he accomplished. He is another person who has shaped the man I am today.

I don't want anyone to feel slighted because they aren't being mentioned here, but you all were vital in me becoming the man that I am today. All my family and friends had a

hand in my success. I came from an environment where being successful had a different meaning. We just wanted to survive, make sure we had that next meal, and get a decent education. In the end, I think this environment actually benefited us. Don't get me wrong: I would have loved to not have had to sleep on the floor when the gunshots rang out. I would have enjoyed not having things stolen from me by drug addicts. My parents would have loved to not have to bring me up in this type of environment, but I think that it made us all stronger. I believe that because of this, I can take a gamble on starting a new business without stressing out. This is because I've been poor before, and I know that I can make it. When things get tense in a negotiation, I'm not nervous because it was more dangerous to walk to the corner store in my old neighborhood. I can look at things in a more positive manner because I know that things could always be worse. With this attitude, I believe there isn't anything that I can't achieve or overcome.

Today, because of all of you, I am the owner (along with Jillian) of a successful gymnastics business called Prairie Gymnastics Club. We also own the Windy City Invitational, LLC, which is one of the largest gymnastics competitions in the country, hosting over twenty-five hundred athletes from twenty-three different states and Canada. My goal is for this to be the best competition in the country. My dad and I own a real estate investment company (RK3 Investments, LLC), which I hope to leave to Olivia one day. I would like to create one more business though. My family owns a lot of land in Arkansas, which was left to us by my great-grandfather Fred Daniels. I would love to get the family together to clean up the land and create a farming company so the land can provide for my entire family and keep the memory of Fred Daniels alive.

I know that some people would consider me successful, but none of this could have been done

without my "village." I know the title of this book is *Did I Make You Proud?* and people think that I'm asking if they are proud of me. What I really wanted to highlight is how many successful people came from a community who were not supposed to have success. I want to make sure that everyone knows how proud I am of them for making it out of their situation to make a better situation for so many other people. With what we were given, we were set up to fail. We were supposed to give up and give in. The people in my village did the opposite. We took the very things that were supposed to tear us down and used them to build us up. Whether it was my mom, not having her mom to guide her through her late teen years; my Aunt Lue, not having $20 to enroll in college

classes; my Uncle Clay becoming a fireman when the department wasn't hiring Blacks; my dad buying real estate without formal business training; my stepdad, Bubba, starting multiple businesses after growing up on a Mississippi plantation; or myself, by being a Black gymnast in a predominantly white sport and breaking through all of that to own a successful gymnastics club and one of the largest gymnastics competitions in the country.

So many have been able to overcome their life circumstances to become successful when no one thought they could. We had to make a way when others thought there was no way. I am so thankful for everyone who helped me along the way and hope that we can continue to pass some of this knowledge to the next generation of kids from the hood. I don't know about you, but I'm pretty proud of all of us, and I hope I made you proud.

DID I MAKE
YOU PROUD

Did I Make You Proud

Did I Make You Proud

Did I Make You Proud

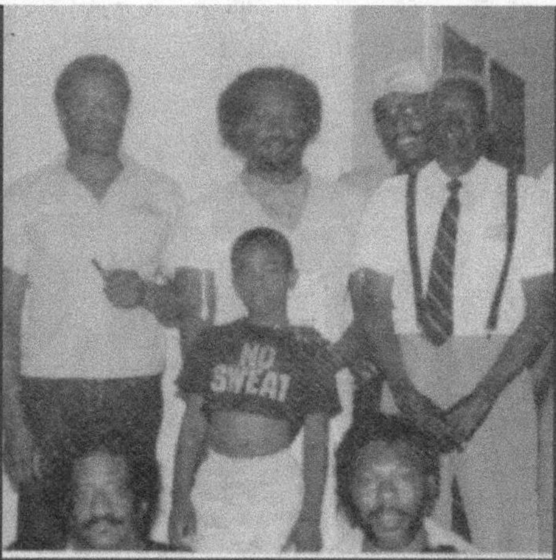
NO SWEAT

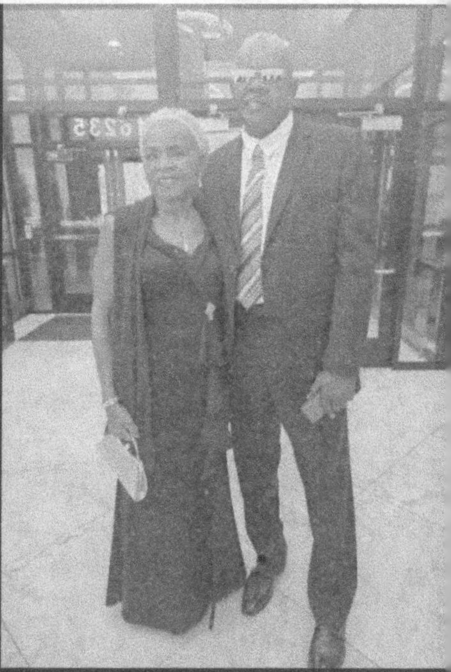

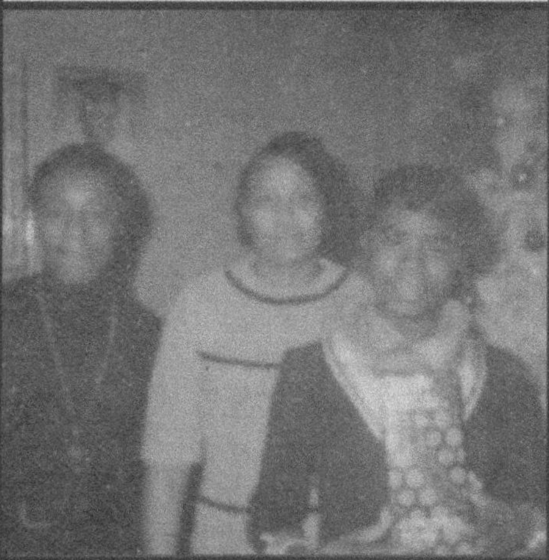

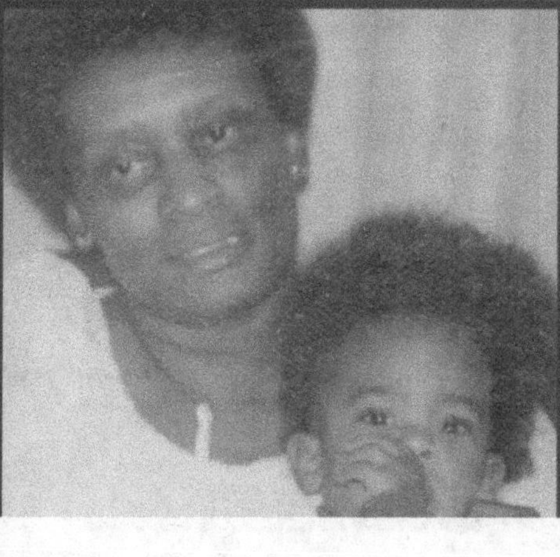

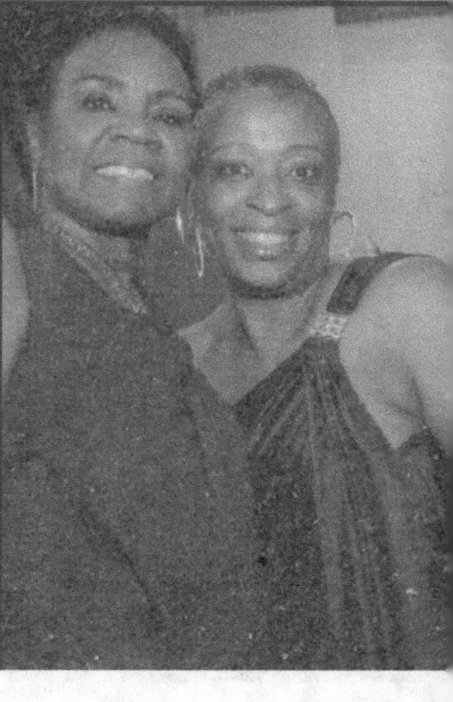

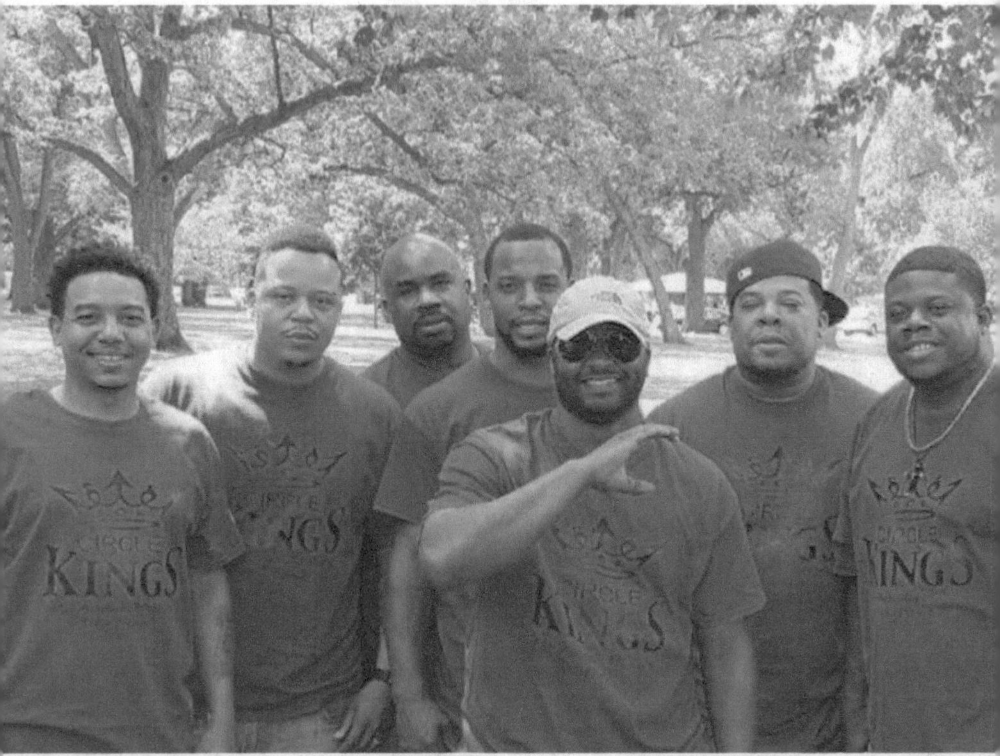
KINGS

NEWSLETTER MAG
MEET DARION KNIGHT
The life of a successful and content author takes dedication, consistency, and determination.
SEASON IV OF THE SHEPUB NETWORK
Who will be the winner of the 2024 ShePub Network Award
DID I MAKE
YOU PROUD
APRIL 2024 SPRING ISSUE

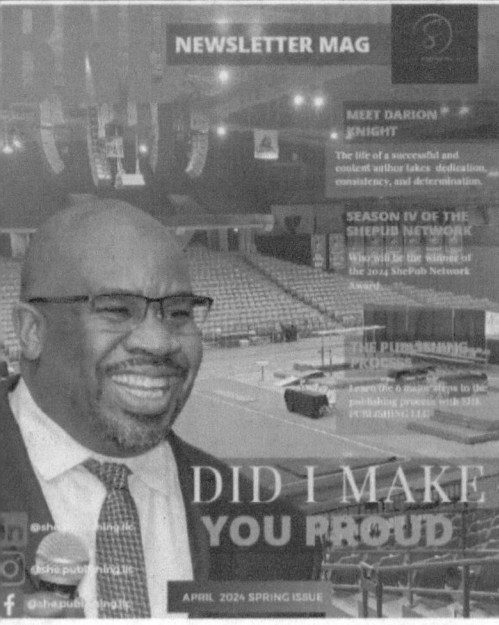

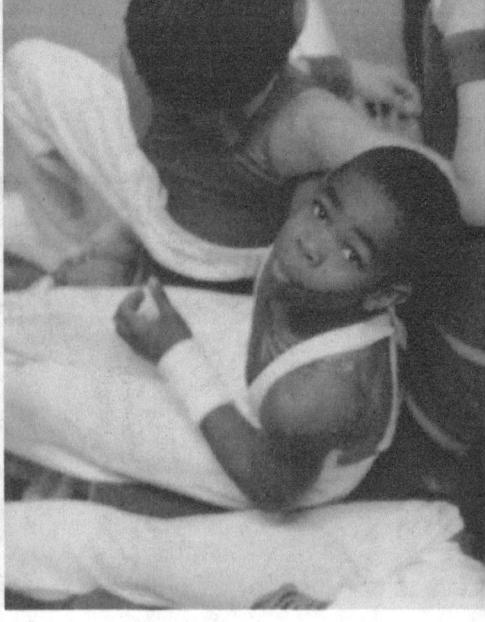